My
Adventures
IN
Broadcasting

A Unique Perspective on Television Coverage
of Major News and Sporting Events

Joe Maltz

iUniverse LLC
Bloomington

MY ADVENTURES IN BROADCASTING
A Unique Perspective on Television Coverage of Major News and Sporting Events

iUniverse books may be ordered through booksellers or by contacting:

iUniverse
1663 Liberty Drive
Bloomington, IN 47403
www.iuniverse.com
1-800-Authors (1-800-288-4677)

Because of the dynamic nature of the Internet, any web addresses or links contained in this book may have changed since publication and may no longer be valid. The views expressed in this work are solely those of the author and do not necessarily reflect the views of the publisher, and the publisher hereby disclaims any responsibility for them.

Any people depicted in stock imagery provided by Thinkstock are models, and such images are being used for illustrative purposes only.

Certain stock imagery © Thinkstock.

ISBN: 978-1-4759-9889-4 (sc)
ISBN: 978-1-4759-9887-0 (hc)
ISBN: 978-1-4759-9888-7 (e)

Library of Congress Control Number: 2013912540

Printed in the United States of America.

iUniverse rev. date: 8/7/2013

Table of Contents

Acknowledgements ix

Introduction xi

1   Education 1

2   Pre-Broadcasting Experience. 5

3   Origin of the American Broadcasting Company..................... 9

4   My first tour at ABC 11

5   "On the Beach"...15

6   Back home at ABC – Interesting People..............................17

7   Interesting Assignments 23

8   1961 My first Airplane Trip - Moscow 27

9   1962 - Cape Canaveral "Mercury" Space Shot.....................45

10   1964 Political Conventions 47

11   Master Control Rebuild...53

12   SMAG..57

13   1968 Political Conventions 59

14   Transition into Management 63

15   1969 -1972 Munich Olympics Planning...............................67

16   Munich Olympics 1972 77

17   1976 Olympic Planning 89

18   Keep Your Mouth Shut!...93

19   Innsbruck Olympics\ Stories...95

20   Montreal Stories 97

21   Fiber Optics..107

22   Lake Placid Olympics..111

23   Planning for 1984 Olympics...125

24   The move to Los Angeles 129

25   Dining with Foreign Broadcasters.......................................133

26   Olympic Experience Cut Short 139

27 I resume my career in New York............................143
28 Interesting and Challenging Projects 145
29 ABC Retirement – New Career 149
30 Consulting Career 151
31 The Grass Valley Group - China Trip 1987.............155
32 Expert Witness...161
33 Videoplex...165
34 Retirement - REALLY......................................167

Photos and Illustrations

The New York Press Orth 25

The Press Orth in use at Ali/Liston boxing match 26

DC7 at JFK Airport 29

View of interior of DC-7 29

A dreary day at Amsterdam Airport 30

"What do we do now?" 32

Interior, Lenin Stadium 34

ABC Control Room in Stadium Entry Ramp 35

Another View of Control Room here 35

World War II Diesel Generator & Engineer 36

Our Hotel 36

Walker by Joe Maltz, cameraman 40

There is no Joe Maltz 49

Graffiti on ceiling of Cow Palace 50

Joe & Jacques on a survey 72

Elizabeth, Jacques Lesguard & Bertram 74

Relationship of ABC Compound to Olympic Village 80

Location of Camera that fed the world 81

ABC Berm Camera shot of Building 31 82

ABC Television Transmission Facilities 84

Flowers in memoriam 87

Transfer of equipment from overturned truck 98

Prosperity Airlines Fleet 112

Sunset-Gower Plot Plan 126

Luncheon with NHK Staff 135

Pettycoat Lane 137

Joe Maltz Engineer 141

Informal dinner in Quangzhou 157

There were many toasts 158

Acknowledgements

My wife Marilyn persevered and encouraged me for several years while I assembled the material for this book. Her excellent memory was invaluable in recalling names, dates and places. Her journalism courses enabled her to proofread the manuscript. She deleted commas where they were inappropriate, added commas where needed and in general did an excellent editing job. Thank you Marilyn.

In 1982 my niece Barbara Schweitzer created a needlepoint as a birthday gift, depicting my broadcasting career. I felt that the needlepoint photo would provide an ideal cover for my book.

Manny Kurtz professionally amended the needlepoint to eliminate any copyright problems

Bob Freeman and Bernie Goldstein for their advice in preparing this manuscript and locating a suitable publisher. Their wives, Rosalie Freeman and Gloria Goldstein read and made valuable suggestions on the content of my book.

Introduction

The question arises, why a book like *My Adventures in Broadcasting* was written? There were several reasons.

I spent forty two years involved in different capacities in the "technical" part of broadcasting. In addition to my normal duties I was involved in the preparation and execution of five Olympic Games, four political conventions and the first coverage of a Russian-American track meet in Moscow. Along the way I had many interesting encounters that had nothing to do with broadcasting as such, but was both interesting and amusing.

I enjoyed relating my broadcast experiences to whoever would listen. My wife Marilyn, who was usually in attendance told me, "Write it down. The stories may be interesting but I'm tired of hearing them." So I started "putting the pen to the paper".

On the bookshelves above my desk are many books about television broadcasting written by many television personalities. These books described their broadcast careers, with their perspectives on the events that they participated in. There was very little written from the perspective of a technical person whose job function enabled these events to be successfully produced and executed. My book attempts to fill this void.

During the process of editing the manuscript I realized that I had omitted several personal stories. The relating of them may come later.

The reader should be advised that there are several typographical and syntax errors. The syntax errors are there because they reflect the way that I related my stories. Marilyn has corrected most of them.

The result, *"My Adventures in Broadcasting"*.

Chapter One
Education

I had always been interested in things technical, even in my early years. Too often I had disassembled and then attempted to re-assemble mechanical devices such as clocks, watches, etc. "to see how they worked". Of course they never worked again and I always had parts left over. In time I did have some success in my endeavors. By the time I reached the age of fourteen I had decided that I wanted to be a "Disk Jockey". No not one that chats on-air, but the person that would spin the platters and maintain the radio equipment. I needed to channel these basic talents that I had inherited from my father and paternal Uncle Eddy.

The process started with my admission to the Brooklyn Technical High School. Brooklyn Tech, as it was commonly referred to was and is, a pre-eminent high school that featured a technical as well as an academic education. My cousin Nat Maltz, a recent Brooklyn Tech graduate, recommended that I apply for admission. I took the entrance exam and was accepted for admission. The technical curriculum at Brooklyn Tech was probably the most important part of my educational experience in spite of my lack of attention to homework, etc. I graduated in January, 1945 with an academic diploma in the Electrical Program.

Immediately after graduation I enlisted in the U.S. Navy. Remember, the United States was at war. After taking and scoring well on several aptitude tests, I was accepted into the prestigious Radar Training Program. After an abbreviated five week boot camp my Navy career consisted of three schools, Pre-Radio (four weeks), Primary Radio (One month) and Secondary Radio (Six months)

The Great Lakes Navy Training Center Boot Camp was located in Illinois on the shores of Lake Michigan. There, I learned how to identify Japanese war planes, tie naval knots, how to march in formation and how to live out of a sea bag.

The Pre-Radio school was located in a former Indiana State National Guard Armory in Michigan City, Indiana. The electricity and basic math subjects were the same as what I had learned at Brooklyn Tech. We were given time off on weekends. All in all it was a pleasant experience.

The Primary Radio School was located in a former Seabee School, (Naval Construction Battalion) in Gulfport, Mississippi. We were taught advanced radio and rudimentary radio repair skills, as well as sheet metal fabrication. This would prove useful in making ship onboard repairs. Again, I had learned much of this in high school.

The three months in Gulfport turned into six months. I had developed a nasal problem and the good naval doctors decided that surgery was necessary. Because this situation developed towards the end of the three month training cycle, I had to repeat this phase of the program.

The last phase of my Navy education was the most valuable. I spent six months at the Naval Research Laboratory in Washington, D.C. where I received advanced radio and Radar training... As you will soon see, my navy experience was more valuable in other ways.

I was discharged from the U.S Navy on July 16, 1946. Now, what to do with the rest of my life? In March of 1947 I enrolled in The Walter Hervey Junior College, an accredited two-year college with a full curriculum of liberal arts and engineering programs.

The school program consisted of five twelve week study semesters and four twelve week work semesters.

The head of the Electronic Engineering Department at Walter Hervey Junior College, Julius Hornung was the author of "Radio Operator's Questions & Answers", the principal review manual for FCC licensing. He had also served as one of the high level officers in the U.S. Navy's Electronic Training Program. Because of my participation in that program, we had a common interest. He had served as a full Commander and I as a Seaman 1st Class. It didn't matter. He took particular interest in my future. Julius Hornung was my first "mentor".

I did very well in all of my classes, and was on the Dean's List three times. I ended up being a Teaching Assistant in several engineering courses. As a result Mr. Hornung recommended me for several interesting work semester jobs. These jobs proved to be invaluable training for my future career at ABC. My first work semester job was as a stock clerk for the Philco Television Service Company. On this job I became familiar with all the parts of a television receiver. On my next work semester I was employed as a Junior Engineer at a company called The Radio Receptor Co. This company manufactured electronic equipment. I was charged with designing and building a device to bond sections of vinyl flooring. It put my knowledge of calculus to the test. In my third and fourth work semesters, I was employed by an entrepreneur named John Porterfield.

This seems to be a good point to start My Adventures in Broadcasting.

Chapter Two

Pre-Broadcasting Experience.

John Porterfield had served in the U.S. Navy and had some connection with Julius Hornung. He was quite an entrepreneur. He had designed the first small illuminated travelling message sign that was used in taverns.

John had an idea of opening a chain of retail stores that sold only television receivers. Remember, this was in 1947. In New York City there were only three television stations, Channel 2-WCBS, Channel 4-WEAF and Channel 5-WABD, owned by Dumont Television Manufacturing Co.

There were very few manufacturers of television receivers at this time. One of the manufacturers was a company called U.S. Television. This company manufactured two television models, a ten inch console Television/Radio/Phonograph and a large self-contained television projection receiver. The projection receiver was designed for bar & grill use.

John sold his first projection receiver to a Bar & Grill on 6th Avenue and 38th Street. The receiver was located in a darkened room at the rear of the barroom with chairs set up audience style. He hired me as a television installer. Salary, $35.00/ week. My job was to install and connect the television antennas and cabling to receive the then three television stations. I also had to provide instructions to the bar owner on how to operate a television receiver.

What an optimist this John Porterfield was! Prior to this job I had never even turned on a TV. However, I did have some knowledge of antenna systems because of my Navy schooling. The antenna installation was complicated because each of the three television stations broadcast from a different location in the city. Television reception in those days required that there be a direct line-of-sight between the television antenna and the television transmitter. I installed two antennas and capitalized on my knowledge of billiards to catch the reflections of the television signals off the corners of the assorted sky-scrapers in the city. I then installed a set of antenna switches and was ready to turn on the television. At this point the bar owner appeared and wanted operating instructions. I told him that I wasn't ready and that I had to make some preliminary adjustments. After I got rid of the owner, I had to figure out how to manipulate the television controls! God bless instruction manuals. I learned that a television set had a Brightness Control, a Contrast Control, a Horizontal Hold Control and all the other knobs that contributed to screwing up a picture if they weren't set properly. After about an hour of trial and error I felt comfortable enough to instruct the owner how to operate the TV. Fortunately for me, the bar owner knew less than me and was impressed with my "knowledge".

I then proceeded to instruct the bar owner in the intricacies of turning on and tuning a television receiver. I played the role of "instructor" for probably the first time. I guess that this was the first time that I used the adage, "If you can't dazzle them with your brilliance, baffle them with your bull s#5t."

I worked for John Porterfield for two semesters. The salary was $35 per week. All went well on the first work semester job for 2-1/2 months. Jobs completed, salary paid. On the next-to-last week of the second work semester with Porterfield, John gave me a check for $35. 1 used that check to pay for a weekend at a hotel in the Catskills. At the end of the next week, my last week on the job, no paycheck. I then received more bad news. The $35 check bounced! I tried to locate Mr.

Porterfield. No luck. I went to court and received a judgment against him. The judgment was useless because John Porterfield couldn't be located. I even went looking for him with a marshal on hand to arrest him. Still, no luck.

The story now skips ahead 50 years, to the summer of 1997.

Marilyn and I 'were visiting friends in Carlsbad, CA. Our hosts invited a former vice-president of ABC, Vern Pointer, to join us for dinner. In the course of conversation, John Porterfield's name came up. Apparently Mr. Pointer had some business dealings with John Porterfield in 1985. Vem Pointer supplied me with John Porterfield's telephone number.

After some "telephone tag" I finally got to speak to John Porterfield! I didn't tell him the real reason for the call and managed to get his address. I then wrote a letter to him and reminded him of the $70 debt. I told him the bad news was that, with interest, he owed me $1,087.00.1 then told him the good news was that I wasn't after the money but 1 wanted to know what happened. I mailed the letter not knowing if J. would get a response.

On the morning of Yom Kippur I received a letter in which John told me that U.S. Television had gone bankrupt and had not paid him any of the money due him. He had no money to pay me and 'was too embarrassed to tell me of his problem. Along with the letter was a postal money order for $70! 1 was flabbergasted. I wrote back to John, saying that it was ironic that I should have received this on Yom Kippur, the Jewish Day of Atonement 1 told him that on this day all debts are paid and all debts are forgiven. 1 had hoped to hear more from John Porterfield. He was a charismatic character and I'm sure he had more situations such as this.

Chapter Three

Origin of the American Broadcasting Company

Whe I started my employment at ABC, their New York broadcast facilities were and still are located on West 66 Street between Central Park West and Columbus Avenue in the borough of Manhattan, New York City. The company was an offshoot of the National Broadcasting Company. NBC was originally composed of two radio networks, Red and Blue. Both networks' New York studios were located in the then RCA building at Radio City. The NBC Red Network was the larger radio network and had affiliate radio stations in many major cities and carried entertainment and music programs. Many of the Red affiliates were high-powered stations and were heard nationwide. The NBC Blue Network was mainly comprised of low powered radio stations and carried news and cultural programs. Abiding by a ruling by the FCC in 1942 to dispose of one of its two networks, NBC sold the Blue Network to Edward Noble, owner of Life Savers Candy and Rexall Drug Stores on October 12, 1943. Initially and for a period of time the ABC radio network operated out of the NBC studios. As far as I know, at that time, Mr. Noble had no plans to have ABC get into the television network business.

The story, as it was told to me, is that Frank Marx, the Vice President of Engineering of the ABC radio network, knew that the

FCC was offering television licenses in major American cities. In 1947, without telling his boss Edward Noble, Frank Marx applied for television licenses for Channel 7 in five major cities where ABC had radio stations: New York, Chicago, Detroit, Los Angeles and San Francisco.

When Mr. Noble found out about this, he promptly fired Frank Marx (and rehired him the next day). Frank Marx now had a lifetime job.

ABC purchased a property on West 66th Street that was previously occupied by a membership riding academy that would serve as the company flagship station. The property consisted of four buildings:

7 West, the members clubhouse housed offices, a studio and transmission facilities,

19 West, the indoor arena was transformed into a technical center and studios.

23 West, the multi-level stable, was converted into scenery storage and workshops

WJZ-TV went "On-The- Air" on April 19, 1948. The television transmitter was located atop the Hotel Pierre. In 1953 when CBS changed their call letters to WCBS-TV, ABC adopted the call letters WABC-TV. In 1949 I purchased my first automobile, a 1949 Chevrolet black Sport Coupe and affixed the WJZ-TV call letters on the windshield. When I started dating Marilyn she was impressed by the logo. I didn't know what she thought. She was impressed. That's all that counted.

Chapter Four

My first tour at ABC

I graduated from the Walter Hervey Junior College on June 8, 1949. Mr. Hornung arranged for an introduction to an official of the broadcast technicians union NABET, who in turn referred me to the American Broadcasting Company's Director of Television Broadcast Operations, William Ahern.

At this point in I should describe the organization of ABC's division, Broadcast Operations and Engineering. The Operations Group, Broadcast Operations & Engineering, was divided into several groups: Studio Operations, Field Operations, Engineering Maintenance, Production Services, Traffic (external communications) and Transmitter Operations. The Engineering Group or, (as their staff preferred, General Engineering). The General Engineering Department had two or three engineers assigned to studio design.

Mr. Ahern interviewed me and did not ask one technical question. If he had, I might not be writing about my ABC career. In any event he told me that he would contact me.

I wasn't sure that I was going to be hired by ABC, so I continued my job search. I was interviewed and hired by the ARMA Corporation, a firm that specialized in electronics for the U.S. government. On the Friday before the Monday that I was to start work at the ARMA Corporation, I received THE call from ABC.

I started work on June 20, 1949 in the Technical Maintenance Department as a Television Receiver Technician. At that time the Television Maintenance Department consisted of about nine people.

The new supervisor was Art Nace. Some of the technicians were: Royce Lavern (Vern) Pointer, Ralph Ilowite, John Serafin, John Irvine, Harold Minnich, Bruce Louden and Glen Burkland (Lard Ass).

I never did get to do any television receiver maintenance. My initial job was as a combination stockman and "gofer". I volunteered for any job that would take me away from belly lugging the heavy field equipment. As a result I became a substitute Mobile Unit Driver. I taught myself how to drive the unit by driving it around the block several times. After clipping the end of the bleacher seats at a Roller Derby pickup, I finally got my judgment on driving clearance down pat. I also went out on microwave pickups to assist the other technicians. After about two months I was assigned to the evening shift. Finally, I could learn something about the television equipment, other than how heavy it was.

My primary function on the evening shift was to respond to trouble calls. One of the first calls came from our main studio. A camera had stopped working. Engineering Maintenance to the rescue! I went to the studio with my trusty toolbox to repair the problem. I opened the side door of the defective camera and probed for the defective component. I found and replaced the defective part, (I've always had a knack for fixing things, sometimes even if they were not broken), closed the camera door, and pronounced the camera as "Okay for service."

I stayed in the studio to watch the action, being new to this field and fascinated by the studio activities. About this time a group of VIP's entered the studio escorted by Frank Marx, the President of ABC Engineering. He was very proud of our new state-of-the-art equipment and wanted to show it off. As luck would have it, he went to the camera that I had just repaired and opened the side door to show his guests the inner workings of a television camera. He didn't expect to see what was lying inside the camera, one of my tools, a "probe". Mr. Marx roared out "who belongs to this?" Of course I kept my mouth shut. I was not going to claim the tool and suffer the abuse that would come with it. The next day I bought a new Soldering Aid. I have a history of losing things. It must be in my "genes".

My primary mentor in the Maintenance Department at this time was Vern Pointer. Vern was a very serious minded individual who didn't know the meaning of "small-talk". He was the shop expert on Synchronizing (Sync) Generators. I must say that he was quite a good teacher, too good! At that time, Vern didn't involve himself in the politics that accompany almost any job tale of how the mix of a mentor that ignores politics and an eager tyro that has no political education or savvy results in a sad situation for the tyro.

As was the usual practice, when I arrived at work at 4:00PM for my evening shift tour, I checked the latest trouble reports. There was one from the WJZ transmitter that one of the two video lines had a problem. I went up to our Master Control Room to investigate the problem. At that time the Master Control had a dual function. The second function was as a control room for our telecine operation. A Group 2 technician, Jack Lupatkin was assigned as video operator for our three Iconoscope film chains. Gil MacDonald was the evening shift Master Control Room Supervisor. He was "God".

Gil had taken a break and left Jack to watch the "store". I showed the trouble report to Jack and asked him whether he knew anything about the problem. Before Jack could respond, Gil returned. Gil took one look at the TR and threw me out of the MCR, without any explanation.

I returned to the Maintenance Shop, wondering what to do about this TR. At this time Vern Pointer entered. I asked him what to do about the TR. "Simple", he stated, "Call the Transmitter." This I did, speaking with the Transmitter Supervisor, Henry Trager. I did not know that there was a feud going on between Henry Trager and

Gil MacDonald and that Henry was a bit of a "worrywart "In no more than 15 minutes, Gil came storming into the maintenance and proceeded to chew my "A—"out for calling the transmitter. Nobody ever told me about the situation between Gil and Henry. Without realizing it I had made an enemy for the rest of my stay at ABC.

The major repercussion came after I was laid off, (My being laid off had nothing to do with Gil. It was strictly "Reverse Seniority.")

In November, 1949 ABC ran into hard times. It was difficult to distribute original "live" programming originating in one of the five owned and operated (O & O) stations. There were only two nationwide cable networks and they were booked solidly by CBS and NBC. The network was rapidly running out of cash. There had to be "belt-tightening". In New York this consisted of reducing the daily on-air broadcasting time to twelve hours and five days a week. Of course the operating staff was reduced on an inverse seniority basis. I was laid off since I was low man on the totem pole.

This came as a surprise since I was told by my immediate supervisor Art Nace that my performance was excellent, (Gil McDonald not withstanding). Based on Art's support, in October I bought a new car, a black Chevy Sport Coupe.

Chapter Five
"On the Beach"

In early 1950 ABC apparently received an infusion of cash and was able to resume a full broadcasting schedule. My problem arose when ABC started rehiring the laid off employees. Gil McDonald, in his capacity as a member of the broadcast technicians union executive board, told management that I was an "undesirable" and I should not be rehired. I didn't know this at the time. I spoke to another member of the executive board and received double-talk. I then spoke to William Ahern, the executive that hired me. He told me of the Union's rejection of me, I also spoke to Art Nace, my supervisor in Maintenance, more double-talk. Gil had done his dirty work. Art was a known drunk. Gil threatened him with disclosure of his drinking if he didn't go along with the "blackballing". Many years later Art confessed to me that he was fearful of his job at the time. In time Art has conquered his drinking problem.

At this point, I thought that my career at ABC was at an end. I took a job as a television serviceman at Davega Stores while I looked for another job in broadcasting. Initially I would be assigned bench work, then a week or two in the field on house calls with a senior technician. I would then get repair assignments in Brooklyn. I specifically requested and was assured that I not be assigned to high crime areas, such as Harlem. After a short period of time I was assigned to a call in Harlem. An incident on that first visit to Harlem convinced me that this job was not for me.

That job came to an end when the company assigned me to service TV receivers in Harlem. That was not part of my employment agreement. After a week of working in this high-crime area, I told my supervisor that I was quitting and the reason for it. He told me that he would re-assign me to "bench" work. Okay. I set myself up on a vacant work bench and started to work on a defective TV. At this point the supervisor came up to me and told me I was fired! Terrific! I could now collect unemployment insurance.

By this time it was late spring and my parents were going up to the Avon Lodge Bungalow Colony in upstate New York. I spent quite some time there working with Meyer (Maj) Newkrug, the owner's son-in-law. I did many odd jobs including driving dump truck hauling gravel and helping to pave the roads within the hotel grounds. I also had time to "play". I shot Skeet with Sid Caeser, who spent quite a bit of time there, having worked there as an MC in the playhouse in his early show business days). All in all, it was a pleasant time.

Chapter 6

Back home at ABC –
Interesting People

Meanwhile, I was still looking for a job in broadcasting. I decided to visit the offices of another broadcast union, with offices in the Empire State Building.

Now Joe Maltz "Luck" comes into play. In the beginning of August of the following year, as I was on my way into the building I literally bumped into Ed Hamilton. Ed had started work at ABC at the same time as I, in a managerial position. We had become good friends. He asked me why I wasn't back at ABC. ABC-TV was hiring many new employees. I didn't tell him what had happened, only that I wasn't rehired.

Ed told me that he was now the Chief Engineer of our local station, WJZ. He told me, "Give me a couple of days and I will get back to you." Several days later I received a called from Merle Worster who was Master Control Supervisor when I was laid off. He had recently been promoted to the position of Network Director of Technical Operations, replacing William Aherne who left the company. Merle was terse in his call to me, "When do you want to come back to work?" he snapped. Merle was like that. I replied, "Tomorrow."He then gave the date, August 15th, to start work. He also told me that I couldn't come back to the Maintenance Department. I said fine. I just wanted to come back to ABC. Needless to say, I was placed back in Maintenance. I guess Gil's influence was waning. Two years later, during one of the many arguments that I had with Gil, he bragged that he got me fired once. (He didn't) and he could do it again. I told him, "Just you try it!" Of course he no longer had any influence in hiring.

I spent the next several years in engineering maintenance "learning my trade." In the ensuing years I was promoted to Assistant Supervisor and then to Supervisor. During these years I had many interesting "people" exchanges. The following stories relate a few of them.

People Stories
Drifting Pedestal

In 1956 the Television Maintenance and Radio Maintenance departments were combined into one, Engineering Maintenance. The supervisory responsibilities were re-arranged to accommodate the supervisors from both old departments. Each shift now had supervisors from both the old Television and Radio Maintenance Departments. It was the responsibility of each supervisor to familiarize himself with both video and audio problems in the television and radio plant.

The term "Drifting Pedestal" can have different meanings. That being said, on with this story.

One evening, I was sharing the supervisory duties with a fellow from Radio, Jim Cook, and nicknamed "Cookie". We reviewed the trouble reports left over from the day shift. Cookie decided that he would like to tour the television studios and check some of the trouble reports. Fine, I would cover the desk and handle any new trouble reports.

After about an hour I began to wonder what had happened to Cookie. I assigned one of the technicians to answer the telephones and set off to find Cookie. My first stop was TV-8. Sure enough, there was Cookie on the studio floor. He was doing something that I considered rather strange. Picture him giving one of the television camera pedestal's a shove and then watching it as it would coast to a stop. He would then repeat the process.

I asked Cookie about what he was doing. He showed me a trouble report that complained about a "drifting" camera pedestal. I had to explain to Cookie that the camera pedestal referred to was not the physical device, but an electronic parameter. After this episode Cookie made certain to review each trouble report with a television maintenance supervisor.

Vonderschmidt/Johnson Encounter
First, thumbnail sketches of the two men:

George Vonderschmidt was a television maintenance technician, with a history of being somewhat racist. He was the shop bigot. I think he hated all ethnic groups except his own. He claimed to hate the Nazis, but I think he was a Nazi at heart. He would sidle up to an Irish Catholic and tell him how he loved the Irish and how bad the Jews and Blacks were. He would put his arm around a Jew and tell him what a good friend of Jews he was. And, of course, he would do the same with the Blacks. Innumerable times he would sidle up to Bill Johnson and extol his love for the Blacks. He told Bill Johnson several times of how he, George, had invited Black visitors to his church to come sit with him. It got to the point that when Bill saw George entering the Radio Maintenance shop, he would run the other way.

Bill Johnson was black, (In those days he was a Negro). Today he would be an African American). He was also employed as a Radio Maintenance Technician. Bill Johnson was a graduate engineer, dignified individual. He had served his time in the army and was discharged as a captain. Did I mention that Bill happened to be black?

Now the story. One morning George had cornered Bill and was about to tell his favorite "Church" story, when Phil Levine happened along. Before George could get started on his "bullshit",

Phil opened up with his own story. The following is, as best as I can remember, Phil's dialogue:

"Bill, did I tell you what happened last week? I was sitting in the front pew of my Synagogue when this "Negro" gentleman came into the room and was standing in the rear looking for a suitable pew. I was sitting up front like I always do, and happened to turn around. and face the entrance, I saw this "Negro" gentleman standing by himself. I promptly stood up and called to this "negro" gentleman. "Hey, .you black bastard. Come sit with me." At this point, George abruptly left the room, never to tell his story again.

Who's the Boss - 1961?

This story illustrates how I maintained my authority as a Union Supervisor in the Engineering Maintenance Department at ABC. The union job classification of a supervisor was a "Group 6".

The day shift of the Engineering Maintenance Department started at 8 A.M. After the staff finished their "coffee and", I would hand out the daily job assignments and the twenty or thirty technicians would go on their way.

Every once in a while the staff had to be reminded of their daily housekeeping chores, like disposing of the empty coffee cups and food wrappers before they leave the maintenance shop.

And so, on this particular morning, I politely informed my crew that they had been negligent in this housekeeping chore, that there is nobody to clean up after them. At this point, one of our newer employee's, Richie Zak, wisecracked "That's what Group 6's are for." Naturally, this broke up the shop. Everybody had a good laugh.

I dismissed the crew except for Richie Zak. Many of the men, of course, had neglected to clean up their coffee cups and wrappers.

After the crew left I set about attending to some paper work, ignoring Richie. Richie kept looking at me, expecting to get a work assignment. I ignored him. Finally, after about fifteen minutes Richie got the idea and proceeded to clean up the shop. When he finished, I told him "That's what Group 6's are for" and dismissed him.

Richie was young and an excellent technician. He just had to learn not to be such a smart ass".

Richie went on to be a supervisor in the then ABC Field Shop. I was reminded of this story when I met him at the ABC "Old Timers'" party, where he received his twenty-five year certificate and gift. I'm sure that he learned that "The Group 6 Is The Boss".

Tom Byrd & Eddy Hughes

One Friday afternoon in the spring of 1962 in the ABC Engineering Maintenance shop, two black men stopped in and inquired if there were any openings for vacation relief positions. Both of the men were well spoken and were well dressed, even with shirts and ties and were very polite. I told them that the manager of our department. Herb Reidel was not in that day and that he does the interviewing for jobs. I told them that he would be back on Monday and that they should come back then. On Monday, I told Herb about our visitors and that they would return today. He told me that he had selected the required number of vacation relief people, but that if they returned he would see them anyway. Sure enough, they returned and I sent them into see Herb.

Herb interviewed them and reviewed their applications with me. Their applications were very impressive. Both had graduated from technical schools and had some previous experience. In addition, they presented themselves in a professional manner. We decided that we would hire these fellows in place of two other applicants.

On their first day of work, I introduced them to my own brand of humor. One must remember that this was during the time of black sit-ins and mass demonstrations. We also had a unique situation in the Engineering Maintenance Shop. We recognized that our manpower list included people of many ethnic and religious backgrounds. Over the years many good friendships that crossed all ethnic and religious backgrounds were established that endure to this day. This situation existed because we tolerated no bigotry and also because we made certain that nobody took themselves too seriously.

Back to the story. The newest employees always received the most menial assignments. Tom Byrd and Ed Hughes were in this category. The fact that they were black was of no consequence. We needed some hardware that had to be purchased at a local hardware store. I gave them a list of the required material, some money and instructions, adding, "Don't picket the place, just go in and buy the material"., After doing a "double take" and seeing the smile on my face they took the money and went off on their errand. Tom and Ed turned out to be excellent employees. At the end of the vacation relief season we arranged for them to be kept on as permanent employees.

Many years later after Ed and I had established a good friendship, he told me that Tom and he were sent to ABC by CORE (Congress of Racial Equality) as a test case. If ABC didn't hire them, CORE was going to make a test case. What CORE didn't realize and Tom and Ed found out was that as far as ABC Broadcast Engineering and Operations was concerned your color, ethnic background or religion didn't matter. If you were qualified, you were hired.

Chapter 7
Interesting Assignments

During the earlier days of ABC-TV, the General Engineering Department was staffed by just a few people. On occasion technicians in the Engineering Maintenance Department were called on to review new products and if necessary correct deficiencies in these products.

Special Effects Amplifier

One of these products was a special effects amplifier manufactured by the General Electric Company in 1951. The device was called a Montage Amplifier. It provided, or attempted to provide, two types of picture manipulation. One, from which it derived its name, was to insert part of one television picture into another. The process was to cut a hole in the background picture with the processed information from another picture, usually that of a person, and then insert the second picture (foreground), into the hole in the background picture. (This sounds pretty ancient with today's technology).

The second type of picture manipulation was to provide a transition from one picture by means of a wiping action, either horizontally, vertically, on a diagonal, or any combination thereof. The basic idea of this device was great, but the execution was horrible. Without going into details, the device with its present design was useless.

Ed Hamilton, then the Chief Engineer of our local station, asked me if I could make the unit work properly. Of course I said yes, I was always looking for something challenging to do. The obstacles were many. This was long before solid state devices were introduced and we had no sophisticated test equipment. After several weeks of design changes we finally had a workable unit.

We used it for the first time on a Pat Boone show where Pat appeared to be climbing a rope on the side of a multistory building.

With the Montage Amplifier now in a usable condition, ABC bought many more and installed them in several studios. The Montage Amplifier was in use until ABC converted the plant into color.

During this process Ed taught me how to properly prepare an engineering report. In the following years this knowledge proved invaluable.

New York Press Orth

In 1961, in the black and white vacuum tube days of television, there were no small television cameras. The smallest broadcast camera had to be mounted on a tripod and required two men to carry it. The viewfinder would be installed after the camera was mounted on a tripod. Movement of the camera was limited to where the camera tripod could be maneuvered.

The engineers at ABC's Los Angeles operation had, in order to give the cameraman more maneuverability, created a small hand-held camera by separating the television pickup tube assembly from the bowels of a GE television camera, extended the cable harness to 25 feet, added an optical viewfinder and created, what I believe to be the first broadcast "hand-held" camera. The "Creepy-Peepie", as it was dubbed, was tethered to the carcass of the camera by the cable harness.

There were two problems. The concept was great, but the quality left much to be desired. The second problem was, considering the rivalry between the ABC East Coast and West Coast operations, the "Creepy-Peepy" was an NIH (Not Invented Here) creation. The New York Operations Group was jealous. This situation had to be rectified.

During this period I was the Supervisor of Engineering Maintenance in New York. I had the reputation of being an innovator. Merle Worster, the Director of Technical Operations for the East Coast, asked me if I could come up with a New York alternative for the Creepy Peepy. I agreed and did some research as to what would be required for a suitable hand-held camera. The unit had to have the following features:

1. Light enough to be easily carried and operated by a single cameraman.

2. The camera cable had to be extended to at least 200 feet.

3. An electronic viewfinder would be required.

4. The operating controls had to be easily accessible.

5. The electronics would have to be compatible with the existing Camera Control Units.

After six weeks of design and construction, with the help of Harold Gordon and Bill Wagner, the camera, with all of the above features was used for the first time on an ABC Wide World of Sports television program. I dubbed the camera, the "NY Press Orth".

The New York Press Orth

The NY Press Orth was used at the Russian-American Track meet in Moscow in 1962 and at innumerable sporting events around the world.

The concept was so successful that we had to build a second unit. The intention was to use several of these units at the 1964 political conventions.

However, the phrase NIH (Not Invented Here) came into play. An engineer in the ABC Engineering department could not let the Operations group outshine the Engineering department. Bids were requested of several manufacturers to supply the equivalent of the NY Press Orth. Such was the jealousy of the Engineering department manager Al Malang that his engineers were forbidden to let the manufacturers look at our unit. The results were predictable. The Bendix camera that went into service did not have an electronic viewfinder and many other refinements that were developed because of inputs from the broadcast operations people. In addition, the reliability of these new cameras was horrible, after the conventions, the use of these cameras were discontinued except for fixed, unmanned positions.

The Press Orth in use at Ali/Liston boxing match

The two NY Press Orths continued to be used for several years until they were replaced by color shoulder cameras.

Chapter 8

1961 My first Airplane Trip - Moscow

U ntil 1961 I had never been in an airplane. The closest I had ever come to flying was in 1946. I was attending school at the U.S. Naval Research Lab in Washington, D.C. I had a weekend pass and had planned to spend it at home in Brooklyn. However, the nation's railroads were shut down as a result of a strike. There was a U.S. Naval Air Station just down the road from the Naval Research Lab. that had scheduled several flights to the Naval Air Station at the Floyd Bennett Airfield in Brooklyn. I called home to arrange for my father to pick me up at the airfield. My mother answered the phone and told me that if I boarded an airplane, I shouldn't bother to come home. Being an obedient son, I stayed in Washington.

That experience sort of soured me on flying. As the years went by, I found excuses not to fly. I told myself that if the trip was important enough and I couldn't travel by land, only then I would fly

However, in the spring of 1961, there was a trip that met this requirement. ABC Sports had contracted to televise a Russian/American track meet in Moscow, Russia. This was to be Roone Arledge's first assignment as a Producer for ABC Sports.

A maintenance technician would be required. His role would require the assembly of a portable television production package that would include spare parts as well as any material that the Russians could or would not supply. This included a production console, chairs, soap, towels and even toilet tissue. (I was told that the Russian toilet paper was not very easy on the "tush"). We would also be responsible for the assembly and maintenance of most of the equipment including a 25 kilowatt diesel generator.

The Supervisor of our department had first choice for this assignment. He refused. I think that he was intimidated by the scope of the responsibility. However, I always enjoyed a good challenge.

I assembled and tested the equipment and packed the necessary spare parts and hardware, considering the difference between the European metric and American measurement standards. Figuring that we would have supply problems I also included such incidental supplies as tables, chairs, cleaning materials and toilet tissues.

ABC Sports had made arrangements to charter an airplane large enough to accommodate the ten man crew and 50,000 pounds of equipment that were required for this television pickup. We were told that the airplane would have separate passenger and cargo compartments. Since this trip was outside of the union's jurisdiction, a separate agreement covering work rules were made. The union would waive overtime and penalties for the travel day if we traveled First Class. All other union contract clauses would apply. We were told that the flight time to Amsterdam would be fourteen hours. There would be a short layover and then a four hour flight to Moscow. After arrival in Moscow the Russians would transport the equipment to Lenin Stadium and we would pick up jurisdiction at that time.

On the morning of the flight, Thursday, July 13th, after a restless night I was rather nervous. At the suggestion of my family doctor I took a Phenobarbital tablet. The tablet worked! My jitters calmed down and I was able to present a brave front to Marilyn... I was able to eliminate my concern about flying.

DC7 at JFK Airport

The "first-class" airplane accommodations were nothing more than first-class seats bolted to the metal deck of a KLM cargo DC-7 airplane. Twenty five tons of television equipment, including a surplus twenty five kilowatt U.S. Army diesel generator, occupied the forward section of the airplane. The only separation between the cargo and passenger section was a heavy duty cargo net.

View of interior of DC-7

The webbing was to protect us if the cargo shifted. The Company had promised us first-class accommodations in exchange for a waiver of all travel penalties. When the Union TV crew assembled at Idlewild (JFK) Airport and examined the "first- class "accommodations on the aircraft, they held an impromptu meeting. The Shop Steward declared that the crew would not travel under these conditions and work rules. Ed Hamilton, our Engineer-In-Charge (EIC), after consulting with his superiors, agreed that our time would now be on an elapsed time basis, including two hours travel time from home. The clock would stop when we checked into a hotel in Moscow.

We boarded the airplane and entered into the metal cargo cabin, (we were told that the last passengers were a herd of Italian cattle). The service was indeed first-class. Two stewards were assigned to feed us and take care of our needs. The airline went overboard to supply liquor. I recall seeing a variety of alcoholic beverages situated in a three-foot diameter tub. Of course, everybody started drinking even before the airplane took off. In my case, the combination of Phenobarbital and whisky eliminated all my fears of flying

A dreary day at Amsterdam Airport

Even when one member of our camera crew, in an effort to frighten me, pointed out the flames coming out of the exhaust of the engines, I said, "So what!" After an uneventful fourteen hour flight, except for a cold breakfast, (the cooking facilities conked out), we landed at the airport in Amsterdam, Holland.

We were told that this would be a short layover. The short layover stretched out to ten hours. It seems that the Russians wanted us to transship our equipment onto an Aeroflot airplane. This was impossible because the doors on the Russian airplane were not large enough to accommodate the diesel generator. The Russian representative couldn't understand that our television equipment would not operate on European power. (Remember, this was in 1961.) Finally, I got sort of obnoxious and told him that I needed the generator for my electric razor. I'm sure that this cost us a few hours of delay.

We were issued plastic boarding passes so that we didn't have to be cooped up in the airplane. I learned that Europeans are not as bashful as Americans when it comes to toilet facilities. As I was relieving myself at a urinal, the cleaning lady made me move my feet so that she could sweep the floor. By the way, this was the first time I had seen anybody wearing wood shoes

After about ten hours, we were told that we finally had received clearance to land in Moscow. By this time the clouds had opened up. It was pouring! By now I was sober, with no Phenobarbital to calm me. How could we fly in this kind of weather? It didn't help when I saw the co-pilot arguing with some airport official. Apparently he agreed with me. He didn't want to fly either. Finally I could see that he was being ordered to fly. As he passed me, in boarding the airplane, I could see that he was very unhappy. When the pilot came on board I asked him why the co-pilot was so unhappy, He replied that the co-pilot didn't' want to fly to Moscow. When I questioned the pilot about the weather, he replied, "No problem, we fly right through the rain and up into the sunshine."

Well, we took off, went right through the rain and clouds and after an uneventful four hours later, landed in the Moscow airport.

When we landed in Moscow, we expected to have some sort of a welcoming group to meet us. Our understanding was that after the television equipment was unloaded from the airplane, a detachment of Russian Army troops would load the equipment into trucks and deliver it to the proper location at the Lenin Stadium. Not so!

Nobody met us. After some haggling, a local airport baggage crew unloaded the equipment from the airplane and left it sitting on a loading dock next to a WW II pre-fabricated hut that served as a freight depot.

Since we had been on the go for 30 hours, it was agreed that Ed Hamilton and most of the crew would go into town. Two of us would stay and watch the equipment, Werner "Wink" Gunther (He spoke German) and me, (I wouldn't leave MY equipment). Ed would send the crew to the hotel and he would try to facilitate the equipment move.

"What do we do now?"

After several hours with no movement, Wink and I decided to try to get the equipment loaded, using good old American strategy. We would try to tip some truck drivers. We flagged down two trucks. Wink, with his German and I with my fractured Yiddish convinced the drivers to load the equipment into their trucks.

At this point, a big beefy Russian lady came storming out of the Quonset hut and with a few well chosen words, chased the truck drivers. They shrugged their shoulders and took off. I guess that the fear of the consequences of their actions was stronger than greed.

Wink and I spent about twelve hours at the airport waiting for transportation. I wandered over to the passenger terminal and had lunch with a group of East German tourists. The tourists were not very complimentary about Russian cleanliness and food. In fact, they were downright nasty.

After about twelve hours, Ed Hamilton and the rest of the crew returned with a convoy of Russian army trucks and soldiers. The soldiers were assigned to load our equipment onto the trucks. I think the soldiers were ordered to inflict as much punishment as possible to our equipment. I kept myself busy, using sign and body language, urging the soldiers to be gentle with the equipment. Fortunately, the only major damage was to a steel camera tripod. The Russians succeeded in breaking one of the legs and snapping the pan head handle mounting.

One of our cameramen, Steve Nickifor, gave me a tough time because I was concerned about damage to the technical equipment. He commented, "So what. If the equipment is damaged, we'll make lots of overtime fixing it." The problem was, he would sit and watch me, on overtime, while I busted my hump repairing the gear.

Interior, Lenin Stadium

After the gear was loaded, a caravan, of cars and trucks headed for the Lenin Stadium. I insisted on riding in the first truck to make sure that we didn't travel too fast and damage more equipment because of the bumpy roads

Our entourage arrived at the stadium shortly before on Friday, July 14th.We were scheduled to start taping the track meet at about 4 PM on Saturday, July 15th We thought that we could unload the equipment, set up and be finished in a couple of hours. The only "fly in the ointment" was that the Russians had unloaded our equipment at the wrong end of the 100,000 seat stadium! As soon as the last piece of equipment was unloaded, the troops disappeared. This was no small arena! At this point our crew got mad. This was the first and maybe last U.S. network pickup of a major sports activity in the Soviet Union. No Russian SOB's were going to prevent us from completing our assignment. In four hours, we belly-lugged all the equipment on hand dollies and trucks completely around the Perimeter of the stadium, set up a makeshift control room and installed thousands of feet of camera cable for our four operating cameras.

ABC Control Room in Stadium Entry Ramp

Another View of Control Room here

World War II Diesel Generator & Engineer

We couldn't turn on the equipment since we had to obtain some fuel for the diesel generator. We decided that we had to wait until morning to get the fuel; we might as well get some rest. We finally checked into the Mockbar (Moscow) hotel at about 4:30 AM and set our alarm clocks for 7:00 AM. At this point, my total elapsed time "on the clock" was about forty-two hours.

Our Hotel

A funny thing happened at 7:00 AM. My room-mate on the trip was Bill Blumel. We agreed that 7:00 would be a good time to get up. At 7:00 AM, the telephone rang. I answered it, expecting Ed Hamilton with a wake-up call. There was nobody on the line. When we dressed, went downstairs and met Ed, I commented that he could have said "Good morning" when he called. Ed said that he didn't know what I was talking about. He didn't place any wake up call.

With all the talk about Russian security, Bill and I decided to test the morning "wake-up" call. That night, when we returned to the hotel and got ready to go to sleep, we held the following (reconstructed) conversation;

Bill. "Joe what time is our Crew Call?"

Joe. "Ed said 7 AM.

Bill. "Then I had better set the alarm clock for 6 AM."

Joe. "Great, good night".

The next morning, promptly at 6 AM, the telephone rang. I picked up the receiver to answer. There was silence. Nobody was on the line. These Russians were certainly accommodating. The bugging of the hotel guest rooms was confirmed by a KLM pilot who told us this story.

The KLM pilots were put up at the National Hotel during their layovers in Moscow. They found that the hotel room toilet flush systems were notoriously deficient. The toilets would back up as often as they would flush properly. On one layover their hotel room toilet was particularly prone to backing up. At this particular time, our pilot friend "blew his stack". He started muttering out loud about the condition of these "blankety blank "toilets. Within five minutes a hotel plumber just "happened to be checking" the toilets in all the hotel rooms. Of course the problem was solved.

Sunday, July 16th

We arrived back at the stadium at about 9:00 AM. For the next seven hours we "worked our asses off" and succeeded in completing the engineering set-up before the track meet started. I think the Russians were surprised that a relatively small group of technicians could put together this operation. For the record, the installation consisted of:

Four RCA TK-31 cameras,

Two Ampex VR-2000 VTRs

Two RCA TS-30 Field Switchers,

Several portable audio consoles and an assortment of monitors.

A 25 KW diesel generator.

Also included were all the necessary tables, chairs, spare equipment, cables, test equipment, tools and assorted hardware that would make this a completely self contained operation. The only two items that we had to buy were diesel fuel and a cover for the fuel tank on the generator. We were able to purchase the fuel but no covers were available. I think one of our Russian friends stole a fuel cap for us.

Interesting Encounter

After I had assembled our diesel generator and turned it on, a short, stocky man with a missing arm approached me. Since neither one of us spoke each other's language, sign language had to suffice. He led me outside of our compound, which was situated in one of the entry tunnels under the grandstands of the stadium, to a sleek looking black truck. He opened up the back of the truck to reveal a 100 kilowatt diesel generator that looked like it just came out of the factory. He then motioned me into the cab of the truck and started up the generator. This was a 1000 amp single phase, 50 Hertz unit. He asked me, using sign language and facial expressions why we didn't use this beautiful generator, rather than that "piece of junk" that we were using. I pointed out to him that while we were pleased that this unit was offered to us, we couldn't use it because of different power standards. This was easy to point out because the frequency meter on the truck had a big "50" on it and I drew a line through the "50" and then drew a "60" in its place. He understood and we became good friends. Even though he knew that we couldn't use his generator, he and the truck stayed with us for the duration.

Joe Maltz – Cameraman.

We had four cameras in various locations in the stadium. Our control room was situated in one of the ramps leading into the stadium. Roone Arledge realized that one of the events, a 10,000 meter "heel-and-toe" race would pass right through the ramp where our control room was located. Roone thought that it would be a great shot of the walkers passing through our control room.

Problem: We had four cameras in operation with a spare camera, spare viewfinder, spare tripod and a spare camera pan head, but no spare cameraman. I suddenly became the fifth cameraman. The trouble was with the equipment. The Russian soldiers who unloaded our equipment had broken one of the legs on the spare tripod and the handle off the pan head. In addition, I had replaced a defective viewfinder with our spare viewfinder.

In order to make this camera serviceable, I had to:

Make a temporary repair to the tripod,

Use the camera rear access doors, in the absence of the camera pan handle, to pan and tilt the camera.

Utilize a spare picture monitor as a viewfinder.

I rehearsed a few camera pans and was ready when the Heel & Toe walkers passed through our control room area.

Incidentally, this camera shot was used in ABC's nomination for an Emmy for unique sports shows.

Walker by Joe Maltz, cameraman

American Ingenuity

As I had mentioned I had brought a variety of equipment and accessories so that we would be self-sustaining. This included tables and folding chairs. The folding chairs had a lip on the rear of the back that, we discovered, was perfect for opening bottles of beer and soda.

The Russians had brought us several cases of soda pop but forgot to bring bottle openers. The men in the crew, without hesitation, opened the bottles using the lip on the folding chairs. While our Russian interpreters were marveling at this "Yankee" ingenuity, the stitching that held the buckle to my leather belt came apart. Without any hesitation, while continuing my conversation with our new friends, I reached into my tool box and took out a tube of "all-purpose" cement. Noting that the Russians were now watching my hands instead of my face, I continued the conversation while gluing the belt together. I applied the glue and squeezed the two parts of the belt together, never looking at it. After a couple of minutes, I gave the belt a "yank". Surprise! The glue held. I nonchalantly closed the belt. The Russians were flabbergasted. Of course I promised to give the glue to our chief interpreter Svetlana, at the conclusion of the games.

Svetlana was disappointed that I couldn't give her the glue right then. I felt that I had to give her some gift. We were using a dry hand cleaner called DIF that had lanolin as one of the ingredients. The lanolin gave the cleaner a very nice aroma and texture. I told Svetlana, our interpreter that DIF also doubled as a facial conditioner and made a gift of a can of it to her.

Since I was the Utility & Maintenance Technician on this television pickup, I was responsible for the setup and knockdown of the control room equipment, Also, at times, I had to go to the different camera positions to maintain and adjust the cameras,

When we completed the recording of the meet, the ABC crew, except for me, went off to the stadium dining room for some well deserved refreshments and a meal. It was my responsibility to shut down and secure the equipment.

When I completed my chores I went to the dining room to join my comrades. Their table was at the other end of the dining room. As I made my way to our table, many of the diners reached up, patted me on the back and congratulated me. By the time that I reached our table I had an entourage of many people who were applauding me.

I asked our interpreter Svetlana, what this was all about. She smiled and told me that they were congratulating me for winning the 1000 meter run. You know, these Americans all look alike.

We finished the knockdown of our equipment Sunday evening. Our visas would expire at midnight Monday. This gave us a full day to tour Moscow, under the watchful eyes of our English speaking guides. Since the Soviets were charging ABC First-Class "Intourist" rates, there was a limo for every three persons. Of course the guide, under instructions from her superiors took us only to those sights that they wanted us to see,

Soviet Intrigue

I saved this story for the last because I thought you might get an idea of the Soviet Cold War intrigue.

The Soviet authorities made certain that we were at the Moscow Airport by midnight Monday.

On the last night of the pickup, one of my assignments was to disassemble the diesel generator and prepare it for shipping. The generator was located outside of the stadium. I was working behind the generator when I saw Svetlana come out of the stadium exit ramp. She was carrying a letter and crying. I watched as she walked to a trash basket, set the letter on fire and dropped it in the basket. Of course I didn't mention this to anybody.

Now, let's "fast forward" to our flight from Amsterdam to New York. After four grueling, (and interesting), days in Moscow, at the very hour that our four day visa expired, we departed for Amsterdam, a scheduled refueling stop, in our chartered DC-7. About midway through the four hour flight, one of the airplane's engines decided to quit. No problem. The DC-7 can fly just as well on three engines. We landed safely in Amsterdam. KLM mechanics would have to replace the engine.

A problem arose for ABC. The NABET technicians were "on the clock". We would have to be paid until we arrived home in the

USA. Ed Hamilton asked us if we would agree to go off the clock until the next day when the flight would be resumed. We would have a chance to tour Amsterdam and have a free evening. The crew agreed. I shared a hotel room with Ed. The next day we were told that the DC-7 would not be available but we would be flying a new DC-8 jetliner. Great!

On the flight, Ed and I sat in the back of the plane, (smoking section, remember that.) Ed decided to light up a cigarette. He took out a book of safety matches, tore out a match, looked inside the matchbook cover, and showed it to me. There was a short penciled note on the flap. As best as I can remember, it read, "Mr. Hamilton, you are a very wise and discreet person." I asked him if it had anything to do with Svetlana and the letter. Quite startled, he asked me, "How did you know about that?"

I then told him about Svetlana and the letter. I described this event to Ed. He then related what led up to this. Svetlana was trying to get Ed to carry a letter from her to somebody in the USA. Ed decided not to do this, being well aware of the warnings that the U.S. State Department had given us not to get involved with Russian citizens. He was afraid that if the Russian Airport Police found this letter on his person, he would be placed in a very compromising position. When he refused to accept the letter, she burned it

Svetlana was a very charming lady and sought to ingratiate herself with Ed. However, he, as well as the rest of the crew was warned not to get involved on a personal basis with any Russian.

One instance of her efforts comes to mind. Several members of our technical crew stayed at the stadium after the day's events to attend to some of the technical problems. There were six crew members, Ed, and Svetlana. Svetlana had dismissed the drivers of several of the cars at our disposal, leaving one small five passenger auto along with a driver.

When we finished our work at the stadium and it was time to return to the hotel, nine people had to squeeze into this little car which was the equivalent of a compact vehicle. The seating plan was as follows: Three people sat on the rear seat with three people sitting on their laps. Ed sat in the front passenger seat with Svetlana on his lap. I ended up sitting on the lap of the middle passenger in the rear seat. I found myself in a very cramped position, with my head thrust forward into the front section of the car, with my face just short of touching Ed's head. Svetlana, sitting on Ed's lap, had her arm around his neck. I watched as she started to stroke his neck and then make circles around his ear. I could see a red flush creep up Ed's neck and then envelop his face. Of course I said nothing, and dismissed it from my mind. Ed was extremely fortunate that he did not succumb to Svetlana's charm

The flight from Amsterdam to the U.S. was uneventful. We stopped at Shannon Airport in Ireland for refueling. The stopover provided us with an opportunity to do some real duty-free shopping at the airport. I also had a great photo of my friend Bill Morris kissing the "old Sod".

ABC News had made special provisions for us to clear customs when we arrived at JFK. All of our luggage was loaded on a dolly which followed us as we went through Customs and Immigration. We passed alongside what appeared to be a man dozing at a desk. As the dolly passed the desk, the "sleeping" man suddenly put his hand up and told the porter to stop. He then took a hand Geiger counter and proceeded to scan the entire luggage on the dolly. He instructed the porter to keep removing each piece of luggage until he came to the "suspicious" item, Steve Nikifor's attaché case. Now you have to understand that Steve was born in Poland. He was scared! The Customs agent instructed Steve to open the Attaché case so that the contents could be scanned for radio=active material. The culprit was Steve's alarm clock!

So ends the story of my first airplane flight.

Chapter 9

1962 - Cape Canaveral "Mercury" Space Shot

In the early 1960's, the United States was actively pursuing space exploration. These major news events warranted extensive coverage by the television networks. The ABC coverage was organized by the News Department and BO&E Operations Group. The Engineering Maintenance Department supplied manpower to maintain the mobile units that were assigned under the supervision of Operations Technical Directors.

In my capacity as Engineering Maintenance Supervisor, I would assign technicians, on a rotating basis, for these "plum" jobs. After awhile, I felt that I would like to participate in one of these space liftoffs. However, since there was no need for any additional supervisors, I would have to go as a technician. This didn't bother me since I felt that technically I could hold my own.

So in March, 1963, for the Gordon Cooper Space Lift-Off, I assigned Keith Lyman and myself. Keith was to be assigned to the Mercury Control Center and I was assigned to the "Pie Wagon". The Pie Wagon would be a field assembled two camera mobile unit. The equipment was to be installed in a panel truck that resembled "Mrs. Wagner's Pie Wagons. " This mobile unit was assigned to provide "Pool" live television coverage for three pre-lift-off events.

1. Gordon Cooper entering the special transportation bus in the main hanger

2. At the liftoff site Gordon Cooper in his space suit, transferring from the bus to the elevator that would deliver him to the spacecraft.

3. The last stop was at "Roadblock 2" where we would televise the actual liftoff. The "Roadblock" was the nearest unprotected site to the liftoff pad. My trials and tribulations during the construction and trial run period are another story (or stories).

My job on the day of the actual space shot was to assist the cameramen in setting up their cameras and then to stand by in case of technical difficulties. Fortunately, on that day, all of the equipment on the Pie Wagon was functioning properly. At each stop, after the equipment was set up, I was able to observe the liftoff preparations.

The actual on-air coverage of this event was an exciting experience for me. No cameras were permitted due to security measures in effect at the time, so I had to make mental images of each step in this process.

After Gordon Cooper was safely ensconced in the Mercury Module, our mobile unit relocated to an area called the Road Block, 2000 feet from the Gantry. We set up the two cameras, no problem. All of the equipment was operating properly.

I was now free to watch the liftoff. I made up my mind that I was going to fix the moment of liftoff in my mind for "posterity". Just before liftoff, our audio engineer put a microphone in my hand so that he would get an audio pickup. I don't know why he didn't just hang a mike outside the pickup truck. Then, as the spacecraft started its ascent, I muttered to myself, "Look at that son-of-a-bitch go!" After the spacecraft disappeared from view, the Audio Engineer told me, "Joe that was great. We picked up your voice beautifully." I was told that my voice went on the air but was drowned out by the roar of the rocket engine.

Chapter 10
1964 Political Conventions

In1964 the Democratic Convention was to take place in San Francisco, California and the Republican Convention to take place in Atlantic City, New Jersey. The television networks have always considered the political conventions an important exposure to demonstrate their ability to cover important news events. At every convention the major networks would supply "pool" cameras which provided a neutral coverage of the podium and floor of the convention hall in addition to their "unilateral" cameras on the convention floor.

Each major network would construct anchor booths that overlooked the convention floor. The booths were designed so that their commentators could see the proceedings and in turn be viewed by their television audience. They also provided television coverage of each hotel where the major candidates had their headquarters. This was long before the individual state primaries and caucuses came into play.

All of the convention center camera and remote television video and audio feeds required a central control facility. This facility would be the equivalent of a television broadcast station which would include a television switching area (Master Control), video editing and recording areas, a television studio and the all important news gathering area.

In those days the engineering department was rather small and the planning and execution of special events were assigned to the Engineering Operations Department. At that time I was the Union Supervisor of the Engineering Maintenance Department and my friend Rolf Drucker was a Technical Director (Crew Chief and Production Switcher Operator) in the Operations Department.

We were under the supervision of Joe DiGiovanna, a Technical Manager (Management Supervisor of Individual Programs or events). Rolf and I were asked to design, build and install the necessary equipment to support this operation. I supervised the pre-assembly and testing in New York, of the necessary technical equipment.

In San Francisco and Atlantic City Joe DiGiovanna would coordinate our activities with the various convention committees, the other networks and all other outside groups. Rolf would attend to the installation of the ABC Anchor Booth and other operational aspects of the event. I would be responsible for the installation of our central facilities.

Now the stage was set. Our crew arrived in San Francisco with six truckloads of equipment and furniture and started the process of setting up a complete broadcast center in a relatively short period of time. As the work proceeded, many coordinating questions had to be answered: Where are the camera cable drops? Who will accept delivery of equipment? What feeds go where? As each person raised a question, somebody responded, "Ask Joe Maltz."

The only way that I could be contacted, remember this was in the days before cell phones, was by paging me on the convention hall public address system. I don't know how many times I was paged on the P.A. system. It must have been many, many times. Then, people started asking, "Who is Joe Maltz?" Most people in the hall didn't know me. I guess that after awhile people started saying, "There is no Joe Maltz." This notoriety stretched out to the remote venues. Guy Welch, an independent cameraman and an accomplished artist, got caught up in this "fever" and sketched this drawing of "There Is No Joe Maltz" without ever meeting me. He also sketched a larger

panorama of the convention that featured Joe DiGiovanna calling,
"Call Joe Maltz"...

There is no Joe Maltz

My crew got swept into this nonsense. When protest groups started
picketing the Cow Palace with various Placards, my technicians
prepared large signs stating, "THERE IS NO JOE MALTZ" and
joined the protesters outside the arena. They even went so far as
to emblazon these signs on an equipment truck that crossed the
country on the way to Atlantic City for the Democratic convention.
Somebody sent me a picture of the slogan scratched into the ceiling
of the Cow Palace.

Graffiti on ceiling of Cow Palace

But, fame is fleeting. People found out who I was and am. I enjoyed it when my older grandson, Dustin, would ask me, "Who is Joe Maltz?"

"Sex Break"

Joe DiGiavanna was quite a ladies' man and was considered a"Swinger". Prior to our departing for San Francisco, he told me about the good times we would have with the ladies (not our wives) on this trip. I told him, "Forget about it. I have no intention of cheating on Marilyn." His response, "I will get you laid on this trip." I said,"O.K, give it your best shot."

Off we went to San Francisco. Joe "gave it his best shot." After one week in San Francisco he told me that I had to go back to New York to check out a new portable production switcher. He said, "Take as much time as you need."

I returned to New York, took as much time as I needed and then returned to San Francisco. While I was home I visited my mother. She asked, "What are you doing here?" I replied, "I was sent home on a sex break." Marilyn was mortified. She said, "How can you talk to your mother like that"?

Atlantic City Convention

Next stop Atlantic City to cover the Democratic Convention. This time I was able to bring my family with me. My partner in this operation was again Rolf Drucker. As in San Francisco we were a perfect team.

I supervised the Master Control and Transmission Center and Rolf supervised the studio and camera installations.

The caravan of motor trailers carrying the equipment necessary to equip a broadcast center arrived in Atlantic City. . Our intent was to off load the three vans carrying the equipment, cable and hardware that was to be installed in our broadcast center. Obviously we were concerned about the security of our equipment. We inquired about engaging an independent security agency. We were told. "No way! "Too much pilfering by outside groups." The Atlantic City Convention Center had their own security group that would watch over our valuable equipment and supplies.

We delivered all of our supplies and equipment to the floor of the newly constructed studio. I knew that certain equipment would be susceptible to theft, so we had taken certain precautions. Among the goodies that we had were newly developed lightweight nine inch G.E. television receivers. I knew that if we were not careful these would be the first items to be stolen. Therefore I had the receivers packed two each in unmarked cartons. Each carton had an inventory number that was identified in our master inventory list. I further made sure that these "goodie" cartons were not left on the periphery of the studio. but were buried under many other cartons.

After we finished the unloading process, I informed the security people that absolutely no one was to be permitted in the television studio until 8 AM the next morning. We left the studio complex under the security of a convention center guard. Allegedly there were guards on duty all night.

My crew arrived bright and early the next morning to sort out the hundreds of hampers. cartons and assorted studio equipment. Each item was checked against the master inventory list.   Uh Oh. Two cartons were missing. The two missing cartons contained four of the G.E. television receivers. When I complained to the security management all I received was a dumb look. I still marvel as to how these thieves located these unmarked cartons. To this day I am certain that nobody from my

ABC crew was involved in this theft. Of course after this theft we were ever vigilant against petty theft. We hired our own security people who did a fine job.

Everything went well until "knockdown" time. My boss Joe DiGiovanna asked me if my crew could load some window air conditioners from the basement office complex onto one of our vans. He said that since the management people didn't get any over-time and there was no further use for these air conditioners, he had told the managers that they could have the units. I told Joe that I didn't think it was right for my union crew to involve themselves in this move, but that I would help him. Joe agreed and we went down to the lower level to see what would be involved in removing the A/C's from their wall mounts.

Lo and Behold! All of the air conditioners were missing. "Those SOBs did it to us again!" Just at this moment, a garbage truck (with the name ABC Garbage) was pulling up the ramp to leave the complex. We stopped the truck and examined the load in the truck.

Son-of-a-gun. Hidden under some newspapers were all of our missing air conditioners. We knew that we couldn't make too much of a fuss. After all we were on their turf. Joe and I off loaded the air conditioners and let the driver go on his way without the loot.

By now we were very suspicious about everything having to do with security. I kept touring the studio complex making certain that the local workmen knew that they were being watched. During my tour of the radio studio I noticed that a piece of insulation pulled down from the wall and was lying on the floor. It made quite a large pile for one piece of insulation. I lifted the insulation and, what do you know, there was an IBM electric typewriter, (remember this was pre-computer days).

Of course we removed the typewriter. I don't know how much material was pilfered from the other media groups covering the convention, but I suspect that ABC wasn't the only victim. I guess some people couldn't wait until gambling was legalized in Atlantic City to start relieving people of their assets.

Chapter 11
Master Control Rebuild

It was rather difficult to settle down when I returned to New York. I was separated from my normal duties as Supervisor of Engineering Maintenance for the better part of a year. My involvement with the two conventions had been all consuming. Joe DiGiovanna had pretty much left me on my own. There was very little direct supervision. I enjoyed the freedom to make decisions based on my own judgment.

There was some conflict between Herb Reidel, the department manager and me. I guess that I didn't realize it, but I resented losing my freedom of decision making. Also, Herb thought that I was after his job. Not true but I guess that was the impression that I gave him.

In an effort to get me out of his shop, he asked me if I would go on detached duty and supervise the rebuilding of the television Master Control facility. This project had been long overdue. The folks in the Engineering Department had been stalling because of the complexity of the project.

The goal was to replace all vacuum tube equipment with the then new state-of-the art transistorized equipment. In effect, the present Master Control facilities would be rebuilt. During the construction period the facility must remain functional. Everybody was satisfied. The Engineering Department was off the hook. Herb got rid of me. And, best of all, I had a challenging project.

I asked for and got several key technicians assigned to the project: Joe Brady, Keith Lyman, Lou Totone and Gene Doran. I moved out of Engineering Maintenance and set up shop in Master Control. Bud Caffery, the MCR Supervisor gave me a corner of the room, provided a desk, and swindled a private telephone number for me. That number, 727, stayed with me for many years.

The rebuilding job was complicated. We had to build a complete new operating system and implement it while staying on the air. At this point I won't go into any of the details. (Reader be relieved) However, there was one situation that I would like to relate.

Some equipment racks contained vacuum tube equipment that carried the entire network audio. The racks had to be relocated so that the new main switching console could be installed in its place. The logical and easy way to prepare for this move was to come in at midnight after "Sign-Off" and then disconnect and relocate the A.C. power outlets. Then the next midnight crew would relocate the equipment racks. As always, I never enjoyed working midnights. I thought that if I could make this power switch during the day, I wouldn't have to come in at midnight. I checked the power cabling and found that all of the equipment in these racks had their power supplied through ordinary AC power plugs.

I figured that if I provided alternate temporary A.C. outlets that this equipment could plug into and did this during the day, when we weren't feeding the Network, there would only be a momentary loss of program transmission. Even though the old tube equipment would lose power for a few seconds it would function since it took a little time for the vacuum tubes to cool down and stop working.

The building maintenance staff provided temporary A C power receptacles. That afternoon at about 2:00 PM I stationed Keith Lyman at the back of the audio equipment racks. When the local station "went to black" (this to allow the local stations to insert their commercial advertizing), I told Keith to move the AC power cables to the new temporary power source. I watched the Audio

Meters dip and then recover. Success! I never told anybody about this operation.

Because of this power transfer we were able to speed up the replacement of the vacuum tube audio amplifiers with solid state amplifiers.

A couple of weeks later, Merle Worster, the Network Director of Operations, stopped by and asked the Master Control Supervisor Bud Caffery, "When will the new switcher be operational?" Bud told him that we were on the air with the new equipment for several days.

Chapter 12
SMAG

In 1965, during the period that my team of technicians and I were rebuilding the ABC Master Control Transmission Room, Engineering Management recognized that there was a need for a department to do specialized design and installation work in the ABC studios.

I was asked to organize this department, with the title of Manager of Systems Maintenance Assembly Group. There was quite a discussion as to what the name of this department should be. It would be a subset of the Engineering Department (which was non-union) but the manpower would be doing "hands-on" work on the equipment and had to be covered by the union contract. The powers that be decided on the following name:

Systems, since it was part of the Systems Engineering Department.

Maintenance, since maintenance was a union function.

Assembly, since the role of the department was to assemble studios and equipment.

Group, because it was a Group. Hence the acronym **SMAG**

I was offered the job to manage this new department. I refused since the offered salary was many thousands of dollars less than my salary as a union supervisor (which included overtime pay). Frank Haney, the Engineering Department General Manager, decided not to hire a manager for this department. I was given "First refusal" for the manager's job if Frank was forced to make a decision and fill the job of manager. He never did.

My assignment was to create and run this new department. As part of my duties, I had to specify the equipment and tools that this group would require to fulfill this new role. The equipment included fabricating equipment and sophisticated test equipment to cope with the demanding requirements of the new state-of-the art color studios that we would install.

I headed this department for 3-1/2 years until I entered the Engineering Department as a Senior Engineer.

It's interesting to note that the SMAG department is still functioning after 46 years,

Chapter 13
1968 Political Conventions

E arly in 1968 I was assigned the task of designing, assembling and building the necessary equipment for the ABC-TV broadcasting centers at the two political conventions to be held in Miami and Chicago. This was in addition to my job as Supervisor of SMAG.

Working evenings after our daytime duties, along with a small group of technicians, we assembled the necessary technical equipment, enough to fill several semi-trailer trucks.

Marilyn and our three children joined me in Miami. I was offered a suite in the Hilton Hotel on Collins Avenue in downtown Miami Beach but Marilyn and I felt that a beachfront motel was more suitable for our family. We were able to secure a four-room apartment at The New Surf 88 Motel. The motel was located on the beach and provided amenities that would suit our needs. I could attend to my job knowing that Marilyn and our children were well taken care of.

The installation and operation went well except for a collapsed studio ceiling that happened shortly before the convention opened. It was quickly rebuilt before the first day of the convention.

The Republican National Convention had completed its run from August 5th to August 8th. The Democratic Convention was scheduled to start August 26th. Eighteen days to knock down our Miami Beach installation, load the vans, make the 1400 mile trip to Chicago and complete our installation! It was a challenging situation.

Joe DiGiavanna, our EIC (Engineer in Charge) was concerned because Rolf Drucker, my co-supervisor, had to return to New York for personal reasons. The total move and installation was to be my responsibility. I was confident of my ability to run the operation, after having the experience of three political conventions.

In Miami, as soon as the television coverage went off the air, we started and completed the knockdown and loading of several vanloads of equipment in several hours. All the vehicles were on the road in record time.

In the meantime, the physical construction of the technical complex in Chicago was being completed under the supervision of another technical manager, Joe Carr.

Chicago Convention

We were greeted in Chicago with labor union problems. Chicago was dominated by some very strong labor unions. One of the largest and most influential was the IBEW (International Brotherhood of Electrical Workers). Their position was that all technical installations including camera cables had to be installed and connected by members of the IBEW. ABC and NBC technicians were represented by an independent union, NABET, (National Association of Employees and Technicians); The CBS technicians were represented by a small union affiliated with the IBEW.

The three major broadcast networks arranged to have CBS install and operate the pool operation that provided basic convention coverage. The other networks would contribute manpower, which included NABET represented personnel and equipment to this basic coverage.

Naturally, the IBEW union objected. There were stories of electricians chopping camera cables with fire axes at some of the hotels housing the delegates and candidates. At the Convention

Center, located in the sweet? smelling Chicago Stockyards, we were instructed to start our installation using our staff manpower who were members of NABET. The IBEW electricians objected and walked off the job. No matter. We continued with our cable pulling and other installation work.

Suddenly, we lost all electric power in the convention hall, including the work lights. It seemed that the electricians were going to try to make our installation impossible. I was prepared. I distributed electric lanterns to my supervisors and armed our workers with metal pipes, (normally used to hang television studio lamps.), as we tried to continue our installation work. Since it was a construction site we were already wearing construction helmets. My attic contains an assortment of these chapeaux. It was quite a sight, with our people wearing helmets, armed with metal pipes and working in the dark

After some time, the NABET union president Jim Nolan, told us to stop the installation work but not to leave the premises. It was eerie, six or seven men sitting in the dark, wearing helmets and armed with metal pipes, not knowing what to expect. After about an hour of this standoff, we were instructed to leave the premises and went back to our hotels.

The next day, we were told that we could go back to work. It seems that President Johnson had sent word to the President of the IBEW International Union and told him, that these union problems were embarrassing to the Democratic Administration.

The problem disappeared. The installation was completed and television coverage went on the air as scheduled.

This was not a serene convention. It was during the Vietnam War controversy. Many factions, including what was to be known as the Chicago Seven, converged on Chicago to demonstrate their opposition to the war. At the time, Chicago was governed by conservative Mayor Richard Daley, who would brook no nonsense from the demonstrators.

It was a setting for disaster. The demonstrators were anxious to make headlines. The police were not prepared for the intensity of the demonstrations and over-reacted. Of course the television networks didn't help matters any. I know of at least one case where one of our minivan camera crews staged a demonstration in Grant Park that I believe grew into a major riot.

I was fortunate to be assigned to the Convention Hall, away from downtown Chicago where many of the riots took place. The Stockyards looked like a fortress with armed police and guards surrounding the hall. I was not terribly unhappy when this convention was over.

The knockdown of the equipment at the Convention Hall was to be completed by Thursday, August 29th. ABC had committed most of the equipment from the convention to be used at the Olympic Games that were to be held in Mexico City, opening ceremonies on October 12th. It was imperative that the equipment from the convention be shipped as soon as possible, to Mexico City.

I was to share the knockdown supervisory duties with a Technical Director who shall remain nameless as well as the management people assigned to overall supervision. This was not going to be easy. The Technical Director celebrated too much and couldn't be located. The Technical Managers also disappeared from the scene. It was left to me to organize the knockdown and loading of the Mexico bound trucks. It would be impossible for me to get the trucks on their way to Mexico by Thursday or Friday or Saturday. Sunday was the day that we finally got all the equipment loaded and sent the trucks on their way. I packed my clothes that night and left for home.

The end of this convention also signaled the start of a new phase of my career at ABC.

The original plan was that I would travel home on Friday, have two days off and start my new (non-union) job on Monday as a Senior Engineer in the ABC Engineering Department

One small note. My last two days as a NABET employee were on overtime and golden time. Not a bad finish to my union career.

Chapter 14

Transition into Management

Prior to my departure for Chicago I decided that it was time to make the move into management. I was offered a position in the engineering department as a systems engineer at a reasonable salary.

I discussed this proposal with my co-worker and good friend Rolf Drucker. He told me that after a protracted negotiation he had accepted a position as a Senior Engineer with a starting salary that was $500/year more than the salary that I had accepted. That was okay. No second thoughts on my part.

Shortly after this discussion, Marilyn and I attended a cocktail party that Frank Haney the Manager of Audio/ Video Systems and his wife Denise had given. Frank had decided to leave ABC. During the evening, I had a brief discussion with Vern Pointer who was now Director of Engineering. I told Vern that I knew about Rolf Drucker's new job title and that I was not upset by the difference in pay. Vern then told me that Julie Barnathan told him that Rolf and I will come into the Engineering Department as a team and that we would both receive the same job title and salary. So it turned out that Rolf had negotiated my salary! Thanks to him I had a new title and an increase in salary before I even entered the department.

Two weeks later Rolf changed his mind and decided not to accept the new position. Rolf was a German refugee and needed the security of the union. The new Manager of Audio/Video Systems, Max Berry was not particularly happy with my transfer into the Engineering Department. He didn't like the fact that I didn't have a four year engineering degree. (He was a graduate of Cooper Union.) So my first assignment was relatively minor, even though I had the experience in my previous capacity of participating in the major redesign of the ABC master control facility.

When Rolf Drucker left the Engineering Department ,Jim Baker requested that he take over Rolf's assignment to supervise the installation of the new hi-tech audio//video distribution switcher. I was then assigned to Jim's role in the design and implementation of the new Video Tape Complex

At that time I had no knowledge of videotape recorders or what support facilities were required. However, "Fools rush in, etc." Max Berry gave me the already approved RCF, (Request for Capital Funds) for the new "State of the Art Video Tape Complex." The Engineering Department had requested and the ABC Board of Directors had approved a $900,000 budget for this project. I asked for and received permission to review this RCF. The scope of this project included:

A major relocation of offices and facilities.

A major temporary relocation of existing film and videotape facilities.

Expansion of film facilities.

Create a state of the art videotape Recording and Editing complex.

All this to be accomplished while maintaining normal broadcast operations.

After reviewing the RCF, I came to the conclusion that the approved funds would not even begin to cover the costs of this project.

I informed Max Berry of my conclusions. His response was "Prepare a new Project Analysis."

After much research, I came up with a figure of $2,400,000. The originally approved $900,000 would barely cover the demolition and construction portions of the project! After reviewing the Project Analysis with Max Berry I had to review it with Vern Pointer, Director of Engineering and Merle Worster, Director of Network Operations. The next and most critical review would be with Jules Barnathan, Vice President of Broadcast Operations and Engineering.

"Julie" was noted for his volcanic eruptions of temper when faced with a distasteful situation. In this case, if he approved the new project analysis, he would have to go back to the ABC Corporate Board of Directors, hat in hand, to request an additional $1,500,000 for this project.

Let me set the scene for this crucial meeting. Julie Barnathan's office was rather large, as befitting his position at ABC. His office chair was more like an elevated throne. Directly in front of his desk was a chair with short legs so that the visitor would be forced to look up at Julie. This chair was reserved for the lamb being led to the "slaughter". In this case the lamb was Joe Maltz. Positioned around the room were a couch and several easy chairs occupied by various upper level BO & E executives. They had come to witness the slaughter.

I had prepared extensively for this meeting. I had a stack of back-up documents that measured eight inches high. However, the request for capital funds consisted only of four pages. I had learned the "KISS" principle. Keep it Simple, Stupid."

The sole topic for this meeting was to review the RCF. Julie had great powers of rapid absorption of material. I presented the RCF with a brief description of why it was needed. As we reviewed each page of the RCF he asked one or two questions about specific line items. When he got to the "bottom line", $2,400,000, he fell silent.

Not a word for several minutes. Then very quietly, he said, "O.K., you did your homework. Now, I will do mine."

I think that the audience of BO & E executives was disappointed. Joe Maltz escaped with his life! I think that they developed a new-found respect for me. Julie resubmitted the RCF to the Board of Directors and it was approved. The lesson that I learned, do your homework!

The project was started. I spent some time learning about the requirements of sophisticated videotape recording and editing. The video tape complex consisted of fifteen clean dust free rooms, each of which consisted of two video tape recorders with sophisticated editing facilities. See the Appendix for details.

This project required many trips to various manufacturers including Ampex and The Grass Valley Group, both of which were located in California. These trips were nice "Perks" to this job. This project by itself was a full time job. However, fate decreed otherwise.

Chapter 15
1969 -1972 Munich Olympics Planning

The 1972 Munich Olympics operations team was headed by Phil Levens, Network Director of Operations. He had assigned a Broadcast Operations technical director (Union), Rolf Drucker as the Design Engineer for the Olympics. Among Rolf's credits was design responsibility for several political conventions.

Max Berry, then Manager of Audio/Video Systems for the Engineering Department, objected to the assignment of Rolf. He felt that the responsibility for System Design belonged to the Engineering Department. Phil Levens agreed and asked Max to designate an engineer. Max suggested Hans Schmidt because of his knowledge of the German Language. Phil's' answer. "No way!" Apparently Hans had a way of alienating people. Max then asked Phil for his suggestion. Phil suggested me. I feel one of the reasons for this was that I had always maintained a good relationship with the Operations people and responded to their needs. And so I started on my career in the International Olympic area.

This assignment was going to be both challenging and fascinating. I would supply basic design criteria for both physical construction and technical specifications. I would have final approval on all plans. The Germans would then build our broadcast center based on these plans. This would require several meetings both here and in Germany.

I would have to make many trips to Germany for both planning meetings and to the German manufacturers responsible for building the equipment. I would then have to arrive "on-site " at least six weeks prior to Opening Ceremonies to supervise the final installation and testing of our facilities.

I negotiated the conditions for my participation in this project. Julie agreed that Marilyn and our children could accompany me to Munich. The company would provide me with the cash equivalent for one coach airfare round trip. I would also be provided with the equivalent funds for a room at the Munich Sheraton Hotel for nine weeks. I would make my own arrangements for travel and accommodations for my family and me. Marvin Bader, the Sports Department Business Manager, offered to find accommodations for my family and me. Now I could concentrate on the challenge of designing a world class Olympic broadcast facility for ABC

The Challenge

To say the least, this was an interesting assignment. The Germans insisted that they would provide all of the technical facilities. However, they required some basic drawings which would describe the physical and technical requirements for our "Unilateral" coverage of the games.

I drew up floor plans for our operation, illustrating furniture and basic equipment layouts. These plans would include power (electrical) and air-conditioning requirements.

It was quite a different story with the technical requirements. Since the Europeans had experience with radio broadcasting; they could satisfy our audio system requirements. Not so with the video and communication system requirements. Those systems had to be designed using available equipment that German manufacturers could supply. The equipment would then be assembled in a manner that operationally was compatible to our requirements. The German manufacturers, after many meetings, agreed. The design of the studios followed conventional criteria. I designed the Master Control/ Transmission area to be manpower and equipment efficient and flexible if there were equipment failures. This design would prove beneficial when we had to switch from sports coverage to news coverage.

My First visit to Germany was in the summer of 1969. It was time for our ABC Olympic technical team to meet with the German Olympic Organizing Committee technical team. The ABC Operations and Engineering team consisted of: Julie Barnathan – then Vice-President of ABC Broadcast Operations and Engineering, Phil Levens – then Director of Network Operations,, designated as Overall Engineer In Charge (EIC), Jacques Lesgard – then Director of European Operations for B.O. & E. –to be responsible for field operations (Venues), Fred Schumann- Director Of Production Facilities to be responsible for studio sets, lighting, George Milne would be responsible for Telecommunications in and out of our studios. Joe Maltz – Senior Engineer, to be responsible for the design of the technical facilities of the ABC Broadcast Center.

Julie Barnathan and Phil Levens traveled to Munich for their first meeting with the German Engineers. Jacques Lesgard, our European Manager of Technical Operations joined them. At that time they felt that it was not required that I attend this first meeting. When our team had their first meeting with the Germans they realized that I should be present. I then received a telephone call telling me, "Come to Munich." That evening I took an overnight flight, (Red-Eye), from New York to Munich and went directly to the hotel. The ABC and DOZ (Deutschland Olympic Zentrum)) teams were waiting in a hotel room.

After telling the participants that I had to wash up, etc., I excused myself and went into the bathroom. Interesting, I observed that there were two commodes or so I thought. Since I was an engineer, I had to inspect the two commodes. One was a standard unit. However, the other unit was kind of different. There were three knobs, what function did they serve. I turned one knob, warm water flowed. I turned the second know, cold water flowed. So what was the third knob for? I leaned over the "commode" and turned the third knob. Result! I got a face full of water! This was my introduction to a Bidet!

I roared with laughter, wiped my face and went into the next room to join the meeting. Of course everybody thought that it was very funny. So did I. I believe that this helped set the tone for our excellent relationship with the Germans.

Design Conflict

As I had stated previously the Germans insisted on assembling and installing all the equipment. However they would follow my guidelines. After I completed the basic drawings we would meet regularly, alternately in Munich and New York. After several sessions with modifications and corrections the German engineers would bring the final drawings to New York for final agreement.

After an extended delay they finally arrived with their final drawings. There must have been at least twenty people in attendance at the meeting. After the usual greetings and niceties were attended to we got down to business. I finally was able to see the German version of my plans. After a quick review of the physical layout of the Master Control/ Transmission floor plan, I realized that they had completely changed the location of key staff operating positions which in my opinion would severely hamper the operation of that facility. This was unacceptable! I was visibly upset. The Germans knew it. My bosses knew it. I literally "blew my stack! There was no way that I could accept these plans

I voiced my opinion in no uncertain terms. "We can't live with these plans. This will not work!" Karl-Heinz Reidel, the engineer in charge of the installation, in a calm manner, responded, "Too late to make any changes. " My response, also calmly "I will not be responsible for this." I rose and turned to my bosses and told them, "Please release me from this assignment."

At this point my bosses hustled me out of the room and tried to convince me not to quit the project. After several minutes of discussion and persuasion I agreed that I would remain on the project if a statement was made to the effect that I would not be responsible for any shortcomings of the operation. Phil Levens announced that he would assume full responsibility. I agreed and told them that I would do my best to make this new design layout work. Phil then informed the Germans of our agreement.

Karl-Heinz was quite jovial and suggested that we break for lunch. I told the group that I would skip the luncheon that I would like to review the plans in detail, which I did.

When they returned from lunch I told them that I have a few questions and some assumptions. The questions pointed out the shortcomings of their design and my assumptions that additional manpower and equipment that would be required to make their layout work.

Now it was the Germans time to caucus. After some time they returned to the meeting and agreed to use my room layout. Herr Reidel said that they didn't want me to be unhappy. We continued the planning. It was now necessary for me to make several trips to Europe to work with the various manufacturers on the selection and modification of their equipment.

Jacques Lesgards

Jacques was assigned to accompany me on my European travels. Some background on Jacques Lesgards. This is what he told me about his background: He was born in Paris in 1920. He served in World War II as a pilot and after the war drove race cars. Although he is French born he became a Swiss citizen. He told me this was to benefit his income tax status.

Jacques began his career in broadcasting in 1945 as an audio engineer. From 1961 to 1966, Jacque was chief engineer for Intertel, one of the first outside broadcast production companies in Europe.

In 1964, Intertel provided one of the mobile units used to cover the Winter Olympics in Innsbruck. Austria.

In 1966 he worked as an audio operator for a mobile television unit that a group of Americans had assembled and performed contract work for American broadcasting companies. ABC then hired him to coordinate television pickups for Wide World of Sports'.

In 1971 Lesgards was named European Sports Director for B O & E division of ABC.

I met Jacques on my first trip to Munich in 1969. At that time he was Manager of European Operations for the ABC B.O. & E. We "bonded" immediately and worked together on the ABC coverage on four Olympic Games. He taught me much about European customs, which helped considerably in my travels in Europe and dealing with Europeans. My European adventures at ABC were so much more interesting as a result of my travels with him.

Joe & Jacques on a survey

As part of my job to supervise the engineering part of the Munich Olympic operation, I had to visit several European equipment manufacturers. Of course Jacques would accompany me on these trips.

Sometime in 1970 Jacques reserved a room for me at the Paris Hilton Hotel. Jacques' apartment was around the corner from the hotel. He invited me for dinner on the evening of my arrival. As I was walking down the street where his apartment was located, with the address slip in my hand, a beautiful young lady came up to me and asked me if I was Joe Maltz. She identified herself as Jacqueline Dunn, Jacques Lesgards assistant. My new friend Jacques had arranged for a dinner companion for me!

She escorted me to Jacques and Elizabeth's apartment. It was on the fifth floor of a small building. One of the two terraces' faced the Eiffel Tower. One could almost reach out and touch the tower. This was my real introduction to fine dining in France.

The next morning, Saturday, Jacques and I flew to Frankfurt. On Monday we were to visit a local factory. Jacqueline had made reservations for us at the Frankfurt Intercontinental Hotel.

As our airplane was preparing to land I could see a large sign ""Hotel Intercontinental" off to the East of the airport. After we landed and picked up a rental car, a Mercedes naturally, we headed off to the West, the opposite direction from the hotel. I said nothing. Jacques knew where he was going. After awhile we pulled up in front of an apartment building. All of the lights in the building were off except one on the fifth floor. Jacques entered the building and shortly after that the light went out and Jacques came out with a pretty young lady.

We drove to the hotel and checked in. Since we were pre-registered, all we had to do was sign the register. I looked at my slip. It said "Herr & Frau Maltz". Mr. & Mrs. Maltz! Wait a minute. I looked at Jacques. He then told me, "That's so you won't tell on me."

As we said our "Good nights" I told Jacques that I would meet him Monday morning. I did not want to interfere with their activities on Sunday. They both objected, telling me that I must spend Sunday with them, that they would meet me for breakfast.

On Sunday we spent the day touring Luxemburg. I learned that the young lady was engaged to a medical student. This whole situation was new to me. Apparently, there was a completely different set of rules in Europe for those who want to play around. I also learned that Jacques had lady friends in several cities. Since then, in the ensuing months and years when I spent time in Munich and Innsbruck, I met and socialized with his long-term lady friend "Gogo". Gogo was a passenger agent with Lufthansa Airlines and proved to be very helpful in many cases. Jacques even arranged for her to have a job at the Montreal Olympics.

After their retirement Elizabeth and Jacques moved to Monaco and settled in a beautiful apartment overlooking the Marina where the Grand Prix takes place, In 2001 Marilyn and I visited them and enjoyed lunch with them in their apartment. As usual, they were gracious hosts. Jacques passed away in October 2012 in Monaco at the age of 92.

Elizabeth, Jacques Lesguard & Bertram

"Vice-President Joe Maltz"

During the course of preparation for the Olympic Games I had to make several trips to Munich to check on the progress of the project. On this particular trip I was asked by my German associates if I would like to visit the venue where the Olympic Yacht Races would be held. They were to be held in the harbor and adjacent waters of the city of Kiel, Germany. The host of this venue was the Kieler Yacht Club.

The Germans arranged for the flight to Kiel. We were driven to the Kieler Yacht Club and greeted by the club president. I was introduced as "Herr Joseph Maltz, Vice-President Of the American Broadcasting Company." I was suddenly promoted from my position as a Senior Engineer of the ABC Engineering Department to that of an ABC Vice-President! I suppressed a smile and went along with this sham. (Later on it was explained to me that this was the only way that the German engineers could get to see this venue.) My escort was a lovely young lady. We toured the harbor on the official yacht of the Yacht Club and had a delightful lunch at their club.

I thanked my German friends for a delightful outing.

Five Story House "Ill Repute"

One evening during one of our several trip to Munich Julie asked Phil Levens and me to take a ride with him. If the boss says take a ride with him, you take a ride with him.

We drove into the Schwabing district of Munich, noted for its bohemian atmosphere. We ended up on a street called Hohenstrasse. Julie parked the car and said, "Come on". Nothing else, just "Come on." We followed him as he entered house number (I don't remember the exact number). It was part of a group of attached apartment buildings. The entrance doors were wide open.

We entered the building. The interior was similar to apartment buildings that you would find in any metropolitan city in America. We walked to the rear of the entrance hall and proceeded to climb the stairs. On each floor landing, standing in front of each apartment door, were young ladies dressed shall we say, scantily? This scene was repeated on all five floors. This was a five story Whore House! As we were leaving the building Julie asked a young American soldier, "how was it"? The GI said, "Pretty good. Not too expensive"

We drove back to the hotel in silence. As we were entering the hotel Julie said, "I think I will take a walk." Phil and I entered the hotel and went to our rooms. Julie ??

Chapter 16
Munich Olympics 1972

I n June of 1972 Marilyn, our children and I flew to Europe on Iceland Airlines. We landed in Luxemburg, rented a .station wagon and proceeded on a two week tour through Holland, Belgium, France, Switzerland, Italy, including Venice and then up through Austria to our destination, Munich.

Jacqueline. Dunn asked me for our itinerary and then booked reservations at "family" hotels in each of the cities on our trip. Each night she would call me to confirm the next day's hotel reservation. That was some service!

This included several days at the Residence Marceau, located on Ave. Marceau, a small B &B hotel in Paris. During our stay in Paris the Lesgards invited my family to dinner at their apartment in Paris. When I objected that we were a family of five and that it would be too much trouble, Jacques replied that it would be their pleasure to entertain us. They were charming hosts. Elizabeth had gifts for all of our children and served a gourmet meal. This visit cemented a wonderful relationship.

After motoring through France, Switzerland, Northern Italy and Austria we finally arrived in Munich. We were scheduled to stay at the Munchen Sheraton hotel. When we pulled up at the hotel we were greeted by the Assistant General Manager, Herr Furster. He had been alerted by Jacqueline Dunn. As I had mentioned, she had been tracking us all through Europe. Herr Furster told us that our room is ready.

Hold on! Room? Marvin Bader told me that he had reserved a two room apartment in the hotel. He told me that he had confirmed the arrangements. An investigation revealed that he had indeed sent his request but had never received a confirmation from the hotel.

Herr Furster, realizing the problem, quickly sprung into action. He told two of his managers to vacate a five room apartment in a building located just down the street from the hotel. He assigned them rooms in the hotel. We now had a five room apartment with full hotel service.

We settled in. Marilyn and our children experienced their day to day living in a foreign country and I went about my business making certain that the ABC facility would be functional in time for the start of the games. They did start on time. German attention for detail was working.

Marilyn and the children had left after the first week of the games. They and Marilyn had to start classes. After some objection from Marvin Bader, I moved in to the hotel. Life in Munich had settled down to a daily routine. Each morning I would drive down to the ABC Technical Center at the Olympic Site which was named the "Oberweisenfelder". My responsibility was to check that all facilities were in order so that the day's televising could take place without a hitch. Little did I know what was about to transpire.

September 5, 1972,

7:00 AM. I was in the lobby of the Munchen Sheraton when word came in that something was afoot at the Olympic Village. Arab terrorists had invaded the Israeli athlete's apartment. I decided to take the shuttle bus to the Olympic site, not knowing what I would find there. I don't recall exactly, but there must have been several ABC newsmen and sportscasters on this bus. Everybody was anxious to find out what was happening.

When we arrived at the ABC Compound we were briefed on the situation. The Arab terrorists had indeed invaded the Israeli athletes living quarters in building 31 in the Olympic Village, which was situated next to the ABC compound, separated by a ten foot chain link fence. Gunshots were heard coming from building 31. The only television picture that was available was from a German camera located on the Olympic Tower. More about that later. The terrorists had announced that they were coming out with the hostages at 11 AM. There was a road from building 31 through a gate that ran directly in front of the ABC complex.

There was a collective decision that we must get a camera out there to cover this event. Our two-camera studio was located in the ABC Broadcast Center to the Olympic Village exit road. We decided to get one of the cameras out on this road so that we could get a shot of the terrorists exiting the Olympic Village. The operating crews were not yet on the scene. Apparently nobody had thought to bring them in. The few technical management people on the scene suddenly became news television cameramen. I went outside to survey the situation. As I have described, the road out of the Olympic Village ran directly in front of our studio building. We needed some elevation for the camera. I noticed an ice cream delivery truck in the parking lot adjacent to our complex. It had a nice flat roof, ideal for a camera and tripod. Fortunately, the driver had left the keys in the ignition. I "borrowed" the truck and parked it on the road directly in front of the gate to the Olympic Village. It was agreed that this would make a great shot.

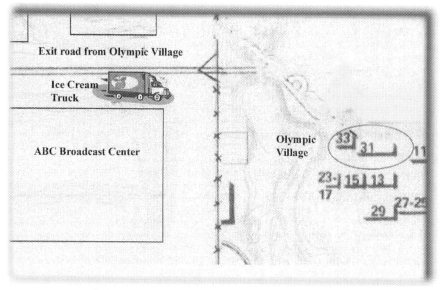

Relationship of ABC Compound to Olympic Village

Phil Levens ABC's Engineer-In-Charge, Chris Evans, a British temporary employee and I moved one of the two camera's, complete with viewfinder, zoom lens and tripod from the ABC studio outside to the Exit road. In 1972 color cameras were rather large and heavy. I climbed up to the roof of the truck and the other fellows passed the equipment to me. We checked the time. It was now about 10:30 AM. I installed the tripod, camera, zoom lens and viewfinder. Phil and Chris extended a camera cable from the studio to the ice cream truck and passed it up to me. By this time it was about 10:45. We had plenty of time. We turned on the camera and made the final adjustments. 10:55! Somebody called up to me, "Joe, its 10:55. The terrorists said that they're coming out shooting at 11:00 AM." With my adrenalin pumping, all I could think and say was "F#%k them". Fortunately for me, the terrorists didn't make good on their threat and did not come out shooting. The ordeal started.

Eleven o'clock passed and the terrorists did not show any signs of leaving Building 31. The camera that we mounted on the ice-cream truck could not get a good shot of Building 31. Its "line-of-sight" was blocked by a berm that was on the perimeter of the Olympic

Village. The berm was intended to give the athletes some measure of privacy. At this point in time the only camera that could pick up Building 31 was located atop the Olympic Tower. That camera did not have a telephoto lens. The best picture that it could provide was a "cover" shot.

We did a quick survey. A camera located atop the berm would give us a close-up shot of Building 31. The berm was located several hundred feet from our television studio. Phil Levens, Chris Evans and I lugged the camera, viewfinder, zoom lens and tripod up the hill. If the situation weren't so serious, it would have been comical, with Phil carrying the component parts in his arms and Chris and I pulling and pushing Phil up this steep hill.

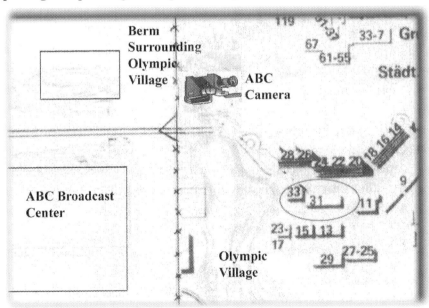

Location of Camera that fed the world

We finally got the camera in place and all the parts assembled. All we needed now was several hundred feet of camera cable. Our television studio, which was constructed by the German television host broadcast operation, DOZ, had two live cameras, each equipped with one length of camera cable. We needed several lengths. I asked our German coordinator, Jurgen Boehmer, for several lengths of cable. He said that he had none. I asked him why he didn't have spare cable. Suppose one of our studio cables failed? At this point he drew himself up and indignantly replied, "Maybe you would like a spare studio?" We were going nowhere fast with this approach. Chris Evens took off to one of the venues where we had similar cameras and soon returned with an ample supply of cable. We turned on the camera and got those sensational close-up pictures of the hooded terrorists on the balcony of Building 31. That camera provided the world with the dramatic pictures of the unfolding tragedy.

ABC Berm Camera shot of Building 31

A consortium of German television networks served as the Host Broadcaster. As such, they provided the basic central technical facilities and studios. Several of the larger countries provided their own unilateral studios, so that they could produce programs that were of specific interest to their viewers at home. Of course ABC had the largest unilateral facility, including our own Master Control Room, since we had the exclusive television and radio rights in the United States.

The only "Pool" camera that was available to all broadcasters was located on the Olympic Tower located on the far side of Building 31. With that camera the only view of Building 31 did not show the unfolding drama.

There was only one usable camera shot of Building 31 and it belonged to ABC. As the hostage drama unfolded, the ABC coverage changed from one of Sports to News. (I believe that it was this coverage that gave Roone Arledge his first taste of television news reporting and started him on his path to take over the ABC News Department.)

We started satellite transmission with Jim McKay acting as news anchor and several ABC sports commentators were now acting as news reporters. Several of the commentators, including Peter Jennings and Howard Cosell, sneaked into the Olympic Village and were giving on-site reports.

Two of ABC's best known journalists, Peter Jennings of ABC News and Howard Cosell of ABC Sports, were able to get past security and positioned themselves directly across the square from Building 31. The problem was how to get their commentary back to our control room to be broadcast to our television audience. They had no portable radio equipment. However there was a German telephone at their location. They placed a call to a telephone at the audio position in our control room. Now the problem was how to get their voices from the German telephone into our audio production console. The German federal telephone service, PT1! forbid using their system for anything but private conversation. There was no time to secure permission from the authorities. Bill Blumel, our Audio Technical Manager, solved the problem by making a temporary connection from the telephone to the patch panel. The audio quality was surprisingly good.

At this time, somebody in the ABC hierarchy made a tactical error. Somebody in the CBS News Department proposed to an individual in the ABC News Department, (I never did find out who the individuals were)), that the events in Munich be treated as a news story and that ABC provide "Pool" coverage.

That individual at ABC didn't realize that ABC was shortly going to lose its access to the only available satellite. We had booked the satellite for a morning transmission and could not extend our time past the expected end of the standard sports broadcast because CBS had previously booked the satellite for a short news segment.

At that appointed time ABC lost its access to the satellite and CBS now had control. As long as they had previously booked the "bird", they could extend their time until our next scheduled transmission, which wouldn't take place until the early evening.

CBS, of course started reporting news of the terrorists holding the Israeli athletes as hostages. They initially used the video feed provided by the Germans, which was not a very informative picture. The CBS people then realized that they had access to the ABC video feed that showed a close up of Building 31. They promptly put it on the air. I don't know if it was legal but they did it.

Crisis Call

I was on duty supervising Master Control operation when a call came in from someone at ABC in New York to our Video Control Room in Munich with the message, "CBS is stealing our video pickup." Upon hearing this, Julie Barnathan came running into our Master Control and yelled, "Kill the feed!" I responded by telling Karl-Heinz Reidel, the German in charge of the facility, to pull the video patch cords. Karl-Heinz hesitated and stated, "Let's discuss this." I shoved him out of the way and pulled the cord myself. Then I told him, "Now we can discuss."

ABC Television Transmission Facilities

At this time, Karl-Heinz came to me and apologized for the difficult time that he had give me in the New York planning meeting. He said that he now realized the reasons for my design of the area.

The crisis was over for the moment. We couldn't get a video feed on the air, but neither could CBS. In the meantime, as a courtesy, we gave the British Broadcasting Corporation (BBC) a feed of our camera pickup.

The panic call came again, CBS has our video feed. It seems that the ingenious people at CBS had picked up the BBC feed in London and fed it via their London satellite. Again, we killed the feed. At this time, Julie had a brilliant idea. He told our Technical Director to put an ABC logo in the picture. At least now the viewers would know whose picture it was.

We put all the video patches back in. CBS put our picture on the air and then pulled it when they realized that they were promoting ABC coverage. I believe that shortly after this charade that the American networks reached some sort of accommodation.

Marilyn's Telephone Call

The news of the terrorists' action spread around the world. Marilyn heard the early report back home in Elmont, N.Y. Since she and our children had spent about six weeks with me in Munich, she was aware of the proximity of the ABC Broadcast Center to the Olympic Village. At this time the news was that the terrorists were going to shoot their way out of the Olympic Village, past our building. She had to get news of my well-being.

To facilitate communications for our television broadcasts, ABC had purchased full time "telephone "tie-lines" between New York and Munich. Marilyn and I spoke almost daily, using the tie-line when it was not in use for business purposes. I had a warm relationship with our telephone operators and they never refused a request for the tie-line. Marilyn called the New York operator and asked her if she had any news of what was going on in Munich. When the operator heard that it was Marilyn Maltz on the line, she said "Just a minute." The next thing that Marilyn knew, she was talking to Phil Levens in our studio control room in Munich. The following conversation, (as related to me by Marilyn) took place;

Marilyn: "How is everything?"

Phil: "Everything's under control. The terrorists had not come out at 11 A.M. as expected and that things are calm right now."

Marilyn: "How are the Jews?"

Phil: "Well, Mark Spitz is back at the Sheraton, under guard"

Marilyn, interrupting Phil: "I mean, how is my husband?"

Phil: "Just a minute." At this point he transferred the call to me in our Master Control.

When I picked up the telephone, I don't know who was more surprised or emotional, Marilyn or me. I told her that everything was okay, that I was safe, etc. It was comforting to know that in the middle of this tense situation, the ABC telephone operators showed their concern for Marilyn and that Phil was considerate enough to let me tie up that critical tie line.

The rest of the story

As we all know, the hostage drama dragged on all day. The terrorists demanded and received two helicopters and with all the hostages, flew to a local NATO airbase. There the tragedy ended with all of the hostages slain.

Flowers in memoriam

The next morning bouquets such as these appeared at many locations throughout the Olympic Site. The games were suspended for one day and then resumed. Most everybody wanted the games to be cancelled but Avery Brundage, the chairman of the Olympic Organizing Committee, insisted that the Games be resumed. The Games resumed but in a very somber mood.

With the games over it was time to return to the United States. As I drove to the Munich Airport I tried to capture the flavor of the countryside knowing that I probably would never return to this part of the world. Little did I know that ABC was negotiating for the rights to the 1976 Winter Olympics in Innsbruck, Austria and that the gateway to Innsbruck was Munich.

Back Home - Settling Accounts

It was time to settle financial accounts. Before I left for Germany I took a $5000 cash advance to cover both personal and business expenses. When I returned to our New York office I collected all my receipts and vouchers, itemized and entered them in the appropriate locations on my expense account form. However, I did not submit the Icelandic Airways receipts since part of my negotiations with our Vice-President Julie Barnathan was that I would receive in cash, the price of a standard unrestricted coach fare on Lufthansa Airlines. The price of the airline fare on Icelandic Airlines to Luxembourg was substantially less than the air fare charged by Lufthansa to Munich, the airline that ABC was using for the Olympics. I included a statement about the travel arrangements that Julie and I agreed to.

I completed my travel voucher and submitted it to my supervisor Max Berry. He approved it and passed it along to the engineering department business manager, Paul Schiraldi. Paul told me that he needed my airline receipt before he could approve the voucher. I told him that that was not part of the deal that I made with Julie. Paul was stubborn. So was I. Since I still had much of my $5000 cash advance that would cover my travels for the foreseeable future, I decided to wait and bide my time.

Paul and I were good friends. We would visit each other and "Schmooze" Some time later, I'm not sure of the exact date, he told me of the deal that he made with technical managers who were assigned to a television pickup in Miami, Florida. He told me that the company would give these managers the equivalent air fare and they could take their private cars to Miami. I said that's a great move and whipped out my Munich voucher. I then told Paul. "I drove to Europe!" Voucher settled, end of story.

Chapter 17
1976 Olympic Planning

After lengthy negotiations with both the Innsbruck Olympic Organizing Committee and the Montreal Olympic Organizing Committee, ABC was awarded the U.S. broadcasting rights for both events. Julie Barnathan's strategy for selling BO&E's services to ABC management for the two Olympics was that we could provide the necessary facilities for less money and more efficiently than outside outfits. I was asked to prepare an engineering budget for the design and construction of a unilateral broadcast technical facility that could satisfy ABC Sports requirements for both Innsbruck and Montreal

After several meetings with ABC Sports Producers and Broadcast Operations personnel, I prepared a budget and a plan which was approved. Our management people liked my concept of creating a flexible broadcast facility.

The 1976 Olympic Plan

The overall design of this broadcast facility had to take into account the physical differences of the geometry of the areas to be allocated to ABC by the Innsbruck and Montreal Olympic Organizing Committees as well as the different technical and power standards.

The Innsbruck Organizing Committee agreed to provide ABC with a large undeveloped area in a building to be constructed for the Winter Games, with no restrictions on the physical layout of the facility. However the Montreal Organizing Committee had given ABC the use of a building on the island that had been used for the 1967 EXPO television facilities. We were restricted as to what physical room alterations could be made.

We were able to solve the space "Geometry" problems by creating a "mock" facility that would accommodate both the Innsbruck and Montreal installations. Since most of the complex cable harnesses interconnecting all facilities would be assembled and tested in New York, precise measurements had to be made on the length of each cable harness so that both plant layouts could be accommodated.

The same equipment and operating consoles would be used at both events. The facilities would be designed to function on both North American and European power and technical standards. The necessary design criteria were completed, specifying and procuring equipment that was capable of operating on both American and European Standards

The complete facility would be assembled, tested and prepared for shipping in New York. The equipment would then be loaded onto six trailer trucks that would be shipped, via freighter, and shipped to Hamburg, Germany and then transported overland to Innsbruck. The equipment would be offloaded and then installed in the International Broadcast Center.

At the completion of the Innsbruck games, the entire facility would be disassembled, packaged for shipping and loaded onto the trucks, along with 40 barrels of prefabricated cable harnesses and then shipped to Montreal, Canada for trans-shipping to Montreal, Canada. The object was to accomplish all of this in such a fashion that the facility could be relatively easily re-installed.

We located an empty warehouse facility one block away from the ABC studios. I dubbed this facility the ABC "Olympic Village". Mock-ups of the two production control rooms, including production consoles and monitor walls were constructed. In addition, cable harnesses that would interconnect all the equipment, in both locations, were assembled and tested.

The name "Olympic Village" was created. In preparation for later Olympics NBC adopted the concept and as far as I know used it for many years and many Olympics.

Planning for this combined Winter and Summer Games proceeded. There were several trips to Vienna, Innsbruck and Montreal for site surveys and to assess construction progress. Finally, in the fall of 1975 we loaded six trucks with equipment, studio sets, etc. and set off for Innsbruck for "Part 1" of our extended coverage of the 1976 Winter and Summer Olympics.

Chapter 18

Keep Your Mouth Shut!

Sometime in 1974, while we were planning for the 1976 Olympics, Phil Levens told me that he and Julie were going to Montreal to meet with somebody from the Canadian Broadcasting Company to discuss the forthcoming Olympics. He told me that it would not be necessary for me to attend this meeting since the topics to be discussed were not in my area of expertise.

On the same day Vern Pointer, our Vice-President of Engineering, asked me to accompany him on a trip to Montreal, to tour the new CBC headquarters. I agreed. This would be a far more enjoyable trip than travelling with Julie Barnathan. Coincidentally, both trips would be on the same day.

Shortly before we were to leave for Montreal, Julie came storming up to me, (that's how he usually approached everybody) and told me that he understood that I was going to Montreal on an inspection trip. He gave me firm orders, "Keep your mouth shut. No Olympic discussions." I said, "Okay".

When Vern and I arrived at the CBC headquarters we were greeted very cordially. After "coffee &", we were given an outline of the day's schedule. Included was lunch at a fine French restaurant. Then off we went on our tour of the broadcast facilities.

Shortly before our entourage was to leave for the restaurant, Julie and Phil came huffing and puffing up to us. Julie told me to leave the tour and to have lunch with him, Phil and somebody from the CBC Olympic team. So off we went to meet this individual.

Where were we to meet him? In the CBC Employees cafeteria,

I was annoyed. I had to give up a fine meal at a terrific restaurant for an institutional type meal in the CBC employee's cafeteria with Julie Barnathan and company.

We picked up our service trays, selected our food and located a table. Julie introduced me to Paul Corio, who was assigned by the CBC (Canadian Broadcast Corporation) as Chief Engineer for the International Broadcast Center Host Operation.

Paul started asking technical questions about the ABC requirements and modus operandi. He must have asked about half a dozen questions and no answers were forthcoming. Julie and Phil kept looking at me for responses. I said nothing. Finally, Julie said, "Joe, answer the man." I replied, "But Julie, you told me to keep my mouth shut." With this, Julie exploded. "G-d dammit, answer him!"

Of course during Paul Corio's questioning, in my mind I was preparing answers. So, at the proper time, without hesitation I answered each of his questions, in detail. Now it was Paul's turn to explode. "I don't need you guys! Joe is the guy that I need! "That started a beautiful friendship that lasted for the entire Olympic period. Of course Julie was pissed at me. So what? I got my revenge for at least one of his "Put Down's".

Chapter 19
Innsbruck Olympics\ Stories

O ne of the "joys" of participating in an Olympic coverage in a foreign country is living in a hotel room for two or three months, with no housekeeping facilities. Not that I have a reputation for doing my own cooking, but it would have been nice to have the facility for a cup of coffee or a cold fruit or drink.

Marvin Bader, the ABC Sports Department Business Manager arranged for a block of rooms on the eighth floor of the Innsbruck Holiday Inn. The rooms were of standard Holiday Inn design. If you woke up in the middle of the night and looked about the room, you could be in New York, L.A. or any airport, anywhere.

One essential feature lacking was a refrigerator so that we could store fresh fruit and cold drinks. Charlie Baldour and I asked Marvin Bader if we could rent some small one cubic foot refrigerators for this purpose. The answer was an emphatic "NO!" This was typical of Marvin. His whole career depended, or so he thought, on keeping "below the line" costs down, while catering to the whims of the ABC Sports production staff. Charlie and I were part of the Broadcast Operations and Engineering Staff, therefore "below the line", therefore no frills such as refrigerators in hotel rooms.

Charlie, other members of our team, and I solved our problem of chilled fresh fruit by filling webbed shopping bags with oranges, apples and other fresh fruit and hanging them outside the hotel room windows. If you stood outside the hotel, you could identify our rooms by the orange colored bags outside of several windows on the eighth floor. This plan worked well, until the temperature fell below freezing. As we all know, defrosted fresh fruit doesn't taste all that well.

This was just another reason why so many people in BO & E came to "love" Marvin.

One of the amenities of the Innsbruck Holiday Inn was the buffet breakfast that was served each morning in the hotel dining room. The food selection was quite extensive; Fresh juice, assorted fresh fruit, eggs, breakfast meats, potatoes, muffins, etc. However, the only dry cereal available was corn flakes. I was trying to keep the same type of breakfast diet that I had at home, that of juice, dry cereal and coffee. The buffet juice and coffee were OK, but corn flakes? That wasn't one of my favorite cereals.

I had prepared for this problem. I had packed several boxes of Heartland cereal for this trip. Each morning I would dole out a portion of Heartland in a sandwich bag and take it down to the dining room and have that as my breakfast.

The dining room hostess was a nice Austrian lady, who would greet each hotel guest as they arrived. Of course she and I would greet each other with the usual "good mornings". She was curious about my little sandwich bag and I told her what it contained. After awhile she would greet me, with a big smile on her face, "Good morning Birdseed Man". Other people picked up on this and also extended the same greeting to me. I didn't mind at all. These exchanges brightened my mornings.

Chapter 20
Montreal Stories

Truck Rollover

The 1976 Winter Olympic Games were over. After a successful operation, six forty-foot truck trailers were loaded with equipment for the trip back to the United States where they would be stored in a bonded warehouse until they could be transported to Montreal.

Why a bonded warehouse? I had worked out an arrangement whereby ABC would pay no sales tax on any equipment purchases until after the equipment was returned to the U.S. and then on a depreciated basis. We would also pay no sales tax on expensed material such as cable, connectors, etc. ABC saved several hundred thousand dollars with this maneuver.

Now, back to this story. The semi-trailers were off loaded on a pier in Bayonne, New Jersey and were to be driven to the bonded warehouse. The trucks had to make a hard right turn on one of the roads leading to the warehouse. It seems that the combination of a top-heavy load (This truck was carrying 40 loaded equipment racks), under-inflated right side tires and a road that had a high crown in the middle, set the stage for a "minor" tragedy. The truck tipped over on its side like a dead elephant!

That morning, at 6:00 AM, I received a crisis call from George Ast, ABC's Director of Purchasing, who was supervising the move.

I told him to make sure that nobody touched anything until I got there. After a hurried trip from my home in Elmont, Long Island, I arrived at the scene, and assumed control of the situation.

Transfer of equipment from overturned truck

The teamsters wanted to get a portable crane and to attempt to right the truck with all the equipment in it. I said "No Way"; the heavy equipment racks would tear the thin skin of the truck apart and add additional damage to the sensitive equipment. I told the crew that I wanted each equipment rack removed from the wrecked trailer by hand and loaded onto the transfer trucks.

One major problem. The trailer had a U.S. Customs Service seal on its doors. By law, a Customs agent had to be there when the seal was broken and give us permission to remove the equipment. Remember, it was under bond for trans-shipment to Canada. After many telephone calls and negotiations with the Customs people, an agent arrived on the scene and broke the seal. The teamsters removed the forty equipment racks one by one, with me hovering over them like a mother hen, and loaded them onto two other trucks for the trip to our SMAG warehouse for inspection and repair.

The equipment was now available for inspection. Since ABC was going to make an insurance claim, the insurance company had an engineer present to substantiate the damage. They wanted to make certain that we did not exaggerate the damage to get an inflated insurance settlement.

This was an interesting sight. Joe Maltz, George Ast, the Insurance Company's engineer and several other people making this inspection of all the equipment racks. It reminded me of a military inspection. As I inspected each piece of equipment, I would make notes in my own version of shorthand. The insurance company's engineer was looking over my shoulder, trying to copy my notes. Finally he asked me, "What does NGF mean?" Simple. I told him that it means "Nish ga falish", Yiddish for "Not so terrible". With that statement the ice was broken. We had established a rapport with the insurance people and a fair settlement was reached.

Disaster turned into good fortune. Because of the truck roll-over accident we were able to transfer the equipment to our "Olympic Village" for repairs. We were also able to make many modifications that I had planned to have done in Montreal and do a far better and less costly job in preparing the equipment for the Summer Olympic Games. All's well that ends well

Gay Encounter

In the spring of 1976, ABC Sports and Engineering personnel were actively engaged in preparations for the 1976 Summer Olympics, to be held in Montreal, Canada. As part of my responsibilities as Manager of Engineering for the ABC Broadcast Center, I had to make periodic inspections on the progress of the construction of the Broadcast Center. This particular trip was at the end of May, 1976. I drove from Long Island to Montreal and planned to return via Albany, New York where my daughter Cindy was attending College.

Since it was the end of her semester, the timing was perfect for me to pick her up and take her home for the summer.

I arrived in Montreal early in the week, attended to my inspection tours and had several meetings with the host broadcasters. By Friday, I had finished with all of my business. I planned to have a quiet dinner, hit the sack early and get an early start in the morning for the drive to Albany.

On Friday afternoon I returned to my hotel, the Holiday Inn-Place Duprey. Much to my surprise I was greeted in the hotel lobby by two of the young men who had worked for us in Innsbruck during the 1976 Winter Olympic Games. Their work in Innsbruck was quite satisfactory and I had told them that if they could find their way to Montreal I would employ them during the games. At this late date I forget their names, so we will call them "Bob" and "Jim". Bob was an itinerant basketball player who played for several European professional basketball teams. He was a lanky fellow, at least six foot six inches tall. Jim was a handsome six-foot "All-American" type. He was a typical college graduate, not yet ready to settle down, who was travelling through Europe picking up odd jobs as he went along. Naturally the "Olympics" drew all types of people as temporary employees, young and old.

As I said earlier, these two fellows were very good workers and didn't cause any problems during the Innsbruck games, so I was very happy to see them. I had planned to eat alone but I knew that these "kids" would enjoy a good meal. I took them to a Jewish style restaurant and treated them to a "Shabbos" meal, matzo ball soup and all.

After the meal, it occurred to me to ask them where they staying. I got the answer, "No place". I made them an offer they couldn't refuse. Stay in my room at the Holiday Inn. They would have to share a bed for one night. After that, they could use my room for a couple of days until I returned from New York. This would save them some money and give them a chance to find suitable accommodations.

We picked up their backpacks at the train station, bought a six-pack of beer and returned to my hotel room. After "schmoozing" for an hour or two, I felt that it was time for me to turn in, since I was going to leave early the next morning for Albany. Since I knew that young people could be night owls and I didn't want to restrict them, I suggested that they go and check out the Montreal night life in the French Quarter. I gave them my key, asked them to be quiet when they returned and chased them out.

About one-thirty in the morning I heard the hotel room door open, some movement in the room, teeth being brushed in the bathroom and two people settling in the other bed. Fine, I thought, now I can go back to sleep and get some rest.

Suddenly, I heard a grunt and then some moaning. I looked over at the other bed and saw two figures "going at it" in the other bed. Oh shit, I thought! "They split up and one of the guys picked up some gal and was using MY hotel room for a shack-up job". I sat up and was about to chase the two of them out of the room when I realized that it wasn't a guy and a gal but TWO GUYS. My two guests were gay, only in those days we called them Homos. Jim was on top and Bob was on the bottom. I could tell because Bob's long legs were hanging off the end of the bed.

What do I do now? I could imagine the newspaper headlines; "Middle-aged American found murdered in his hotel room." I figured that discretion was the better part of valor and covered my head with my blanket. That was the end of my sleep for the night. I tossed and turned for the next couple of hours and finally realized that I was finished with sleep for this night.   I got out of bed and quietly, very quietly, got dressed and left. Besides, I didn't know how I would re-act if I saw them in the morning. I got into my car and left for Albany. After awhile I got rather drowsy and had trouble keeping the car on the road. I pulled off to the side and caught a few zzzz.

I arrived at my daughter's dormitory at about 7 AM, and after much pounding on the door, she opened the door and said "what are you doing here so early?" I mumbled "I'll tell you later. Just let me lie down somewhere and get some shut-eye."

We shared the driving to long Island. Cindy said that I was quite grumpy. I wonder why? When we got home the grumpiness was still evident. Marilyn asked Cindy why was I grumpy. Cindy said, "Ask Dad." She did, and I told her why.

When I returned to Montreal on Monday I wondered if I would find anything amiss in my hotel room. The room was in good order. My personal belongings were intact. The two gays did a fine job for us at the Olympic Games. Jim took up with a young lady that we referred to as "jiggles". I guess he was bi-sexual. I never mentioned this episode to anybody during the games. However, Marilyn spotted them immediately from my description. Off course, she was also discreet.

After the games, when a few of us were relaxing over some cocktails, I related the story to Ben Greenberg, one of my engineers. He was horrified. He said that if he knew about it he wouldn't have been able to look them in the face. I guess that is why I didn't tell anyone.

The lesson that I learned from this is that while these guys were wrong in imposing on my hospitality this way, their personal sexual preferences didn't keep them from doing their jobs in a proper fashion. And with them sleeping in the same bed, they were put in an irresistible situation.

Montreal Studio "Re-Do"

Preparation for the 1976 winter and Summer Olympic Games included consideration of having, as close as possible, identical floor plans for the control rooms and live studio. As described in Chapter17 we accomplished this by constructing mock-ups of the ABC Olympic broadcast center facilities in a loft on West 65th Street in New York.

One challenge was our inability to modify the existing studio layout in the building assigned to us in Montreal. This building was originally used for broadcast coverage of the 1967 Montreal World's fair. We were told that we had to use the studio complex "as is", that is "No modifications of the floor plan." I was stuck with this limitation. There was limited viewing space for the many advertising clients that would attend the Olympics and would like to see our television production "In action". The main control room was too small. We did not have this limitation in the Innsbruck operation. I also had to consider the use of the same prefabricated cables for both Innsbruck and Montreal. With this in mind I kept the operating area of the two control rooms fairly similar in size. This took up a considerable portion of the floor space available in Montreal for the main control room, limiting space for a clients viewing room.

I laid out the main control room in our Olympic Village, showing the difference in the two control rooms. Of course there was a substantial difference in the size of the Clients Observation Rooms.

The ABC Sports production team, which consisted of Roone Arledge, Chuck Howard, Geoff Mason, Marv Bader and their production operating personnel inspected the mock-up of the control room which graphically illustrated the differences between Innsbruck and Montreal. I described the limitations of the Montreal construction. Roone and his team agreed that this was livable. The floor plans were approved and I gave the go ahead for construction to the Host broadcasters in Innsbruck and Montreal.

The operation in Innsbruck was a complete success and we looked forward to a repeat performance in Montreal.

About six weeks before our operation was to start in Montreal, Roone decided to make an inspection of the Montreal facilities. I was not notified of this tour. (I will give Marvin Bader the benefit of doubt that I was not notified). Maybe he couldn't find me, since I had my own schedule to contend with. However, he could have notified Phil

Levens, our overall Engineer-In-Charge. Marvin had his own ideas of what Engineering should know.

Fortunately, I was already in Montreal in the broadcasting center with Ben Greenberg, conducting some technical tests.

Ben and I were conducting our tests, when who should suddenly appear on the scene but Roone and his entourage. They were here to conduct a survey of our facilities. I left Ben Greenberg to continue the technical tests and joined the tour.

The studio complex consisted of the main control room, a small studio storage area, the studio and a small client's booth with a window overlooking the control room and the studio.

Roone approved the studio and the storage area. (Who in the production team could possible care about the storage area?) When he came into the control room he exclaimed, "This will never do! The control room is too small. We must change it." His entourage, including me, followed him into the studio, where he came to the conclusion that we must make the following alterations to the floor plan. Roone's edict; "Convert the storage area into a studio, convert the studio into a control room and make the control room into a client's observation booth."

As I heard his pronouncements, many thoughts ran through my mind. "'He's out of his mind!" All of the power, air conditioning and lighting grids were installed and operational. Why do the clients need such a huge viewing room? One of our objectives was to limit the number of clients in the operating area. A small viewing booth would do just that. How can I convince Arledge to change his mind?'

At this point, I was facing Roone, Chuck Howard, and his Producer with the rest off his entourage behind him. As I was describing my objections to Roone's suggestions, Marvin Bader was waving his arms to get my attention and motioning me to shut up. I ignored Marvin and continued my discussion with Roone.

I asked him what his main objection was. He replied that there was not enough room in the control room to accommodate the necessary production personnel and he needed an observation area for clients. I asked him for some time to solve this problem and he agreed.

Since I had designed the control room so that all of the technical facilities were on one side of the room, it would not be a big deal to expand the other side of the control room to accommodate the production personnel and an observation booth for VIP's. I reviewed this alternative plan with John Weber, the CBC architect assigned to the project. He agreed that it certainly was feasible. However, the stumbling block would be the CBC Olympic executives who were very jealous of their prerogatives. Their egos had to be satisfied. This had to be their idea.

I showed the revised plan to Geoff Mason, one of our producers, and he agreed that Roone would be satisfied with the modified layout. We arranged a meeting with Marius Morais, the executive in charge of the CBC Host Broadcasting Operation. I brought the existing floor plans and left the proposed modified plans in my office.

At the meeting I explained our predicament and described Arledge's' proposal. I showed Marius the existing floor plans and asked if there was anything that he could do to help us. I told him that we needed more space for the production people. Marius saw the obvious and suggested moving one wall. This would entail putting a jog in the hallway behind the studio complex and making two operations offices smaller. At this point John Weber, who was well rehearsed, said that this would be no problem. I told Marius that his idea was great and that he "saved our lives". It was a done deal. Roone was happy. Marius was happy that "his" idea was adopted. And I got off the hook without making expensive changes. Of course this problem never would have arisen if Marius would have let us move the wall in the first place.

Our coverage of The Montreal Games went off without any further problems.

I received an "Emmy" for my engineering work on the 1976 winter and Summer Olympics.

Chapter 21

Fiber Optics

I was introduced to a possible use of fiber optics in 1977 by Eric Rosenthal one of my engineers. The Galileo Company, which specialized in medical optical products that utilized fiber optics to transmit information was interested in expanding their fiber optic market and television broadcasting which seemed to be a logical target.

At that time we were engaged in a project to install several hundred audio and video cables between the ABC Central Switching and several studios. The cable runs were to be at least one thousand feet long.

Unfortunately at that time, we were involved in a strike by the technicians union and all of the engineering staff was pulling double duty, our regular engineering work and operating assignments.

After the strike was settled, we met with the engineers from Galileo to determine what could be done to test fiber optics in the field. Since ABC was scheduled to be the Coordinating Broadcaster at the 1980 Winter Olympics, we decided that Lake Placid would be an ideal testing ground for the use of fiber optics in the television broadcast world.

The plan was to install four multi-mode fibers, (at that time multi-mode fiber was the only game in town), between the ABC

Master Control in the International Broadcast Center, and the Lake Placid Horse Show Grounds, where the Olympic opening ceremony would take place. The distance between the broadcast center and the Horse Show Grounds was about 1500 feet.

Galileo (by now the company had changed its name to The Galite Company) engineers had designed transmit/receive equipment that occupied the better part of a six foot equipment rack. I felt the equipment was too bulky and would not be suited for commercial use.

With the permission of the Galite Company I contacted Bill Riordan, Engineering Vice-President of the Grass Valley Group, the company that was supplying ABC with much of our technical equipment. I asked him if he would be interested in developing a new method of transmitting television audio/video signals that would be demonstrated at the 1980 Winter Olympics. ABC had already given Grass Valley about four million dollars worth of orders for equipment for the game. Bill, a man of few words, replied, "Yes".

Bottom line. Grass Valley delivered. We used four Galite fiber optic circuits between our Olympic Broadcast Center and the Lake Placid Horse Show Grounds where the opening ceremonies took place. Grass Valley Group introduced their new "Wave link" fiber optic modulator and demodulator for this event. This was the start of their fiber optic product line that has been used by many broadcasters. Humph. No royalties for me.

At about the same time, I was approached by Sel Roberts, the Engineering Manager for the New York Telephone Company Olympic Project. Would ABC be interested in a Fiber Optic demonstration project for Lake Placid?

My response was, Okay, there is always room for one more. However, Sel Roberts said that if Bell Labs found out that another company was involved in a similar project, they would cancel out.

We agreed not to say anything to the Telco people about the Galileo/Grass Valley project until it was too late for them to pull out.

Bell Labs developed their own version of a fiber optic transmission system. They installed six fiber optic circuits for use between the broadcast center and the Olympic Ice Skating Rink.

The two separately designed fiber optic systems were the precursor of fiber optic systems and equipment now in use throughout the world.

Chapter 22
Lake Placid Olympics

As previously mentioned, ABC had been awarded the American radio and television broadcast rights to the 1980 Winter Olympics which was to take place in Lake Placid, New York State. One condition was that we would be the Host Broadcaster. That meant that ABC would have the responsibility of providing "neutral" coverage of all fourteen events at five venues in addition to providing the ABC unique coverage featuring American athletes.

I was assigned the job of designing the International Broadcast Center which would include the ABC studios studio and space for foreign broadcasters. The foreign broadcasters would design their own facilities. My design responsibilities would cover video recording and playback of all events and satellite uplink facilities. Quite an assignment! The following stories recount some of my experiences during the run-up to and during the Lake Placid Olympics.

Installation of the ABC Technical Center started in the summer of 1979. This required that I make many trips to the village of Lake Placid. For short visits, the most convenient way was to book flights on a commuter airline with the name of Prosperity Airways. Their "fleet" consisted of one twin engine airplane. I would fly from LaGuardia Airport to a small airport in Saranac Lake, where I would pick up a rental car to complete my trip to Lake Placid

In the course of many flights to and from Saranac Lake I became friendly with the pilots (naturally). In time the trip became rather boring. I would purchase a copy of the New York Times to occupy my time on the trip. In the waiting room at LaGuardia Airport I could always spot the sleek Prosperity airplane landing and taxiing to its parking spot.

Prosperity Airlines Fleet

On this particular day I could not spot the airplane. However, the Co-Pilot suddenly appeared in the waiting room. (Usually, there was a pilot and co-pilot on this flight). The lone pilot announced that due to a maintenance problem the seven passenger airplane was not available and that we would use a smaller five passenger replacement airplane with one pilot. (In retrospect I don't know how legal that was). There were four passengers on this flight, myself and three other people. I didn't know the other passengers. They were apparently traveling together. After the pilot loaded our baggage he asked me if I would like to sit in the co-pilot's seat. Naturally I agreed.

Now, for the first shock. The airplane was obviously twenty or thirty years old, and I mean OLD. The two engines were of the rotary type. The cockpit engine gauges were all of the old-fashioned variety with mechanical couplings to the engines. When the engines were started, they made quite a racket. The needles on the gauges were vibrating all over the place. I commented to the pilot that this appeared to be quite an old airplane. He replied that these airplanes get better as they get older. We immediately got clearance from the control tower. I think the Air Controllers just wanted to get rid of this clunker. As we took off, the pilot, wearing earphones, was in constant conversation with somebody. I think that he needed the earphones because without them he couldn't hear over the noise of these ancient engines.

Normally, by this time, I would be deeply engrossed in my newspaper. But between the noise of the engine, the gauge needles jumping around, the gauge connecting cables vibrating all over the place, the pilot in earnest conversation with somebody and the airplane bouncing up and down, I had no inclination to read my newspaper. I guess that I was kind of concerned or just plain scared. After about ten minutes, the pilot took the airplane to a higher altitude. The vibrations and bouncing ceased. I asked the pilot what all the conversation was about. He told me that there was quite a bit of turbulence at the lower altitude and he was trying to get clearance to get out of the turbulence. The flight settled into a nice comfortable trip. I opened my newspaper and caught up on the news around the world. We landed on time. My car was waiting for me and I drove to the broadcast center in Lake Placid

Later that morning, while I was making my inspection tour of the Center, one of our telecommunication's people asked me if I could spend some time with a few representatives from The New York Telephone Company and give them a tour of our facilities. These were the same people who were on the flight with me! They were as surprised to see me as I was to see them. They told me that on board the airplane they thought that I was a flight inspector of some sort. They were scared out of their wits with the entire goings on in the airplane, but when I started reading my newspaper they figured that everything must be okay

That afternoon I completed my tour of the facilities and drove to the Saranac Airport. I expected to fly to New York on the Prosperity Airlines replacement airplane. I walked out on the tarmac and saw that a couple of mechanics were working on one of the airplane's engines. I asked them what the problem was. They replied that they are trying to figure out the problem. Remember, this "clunker" was the one that we flew on that morning.

With that in mind I went back to the auto rental counter and reclaimed my car. I drove down to Albany and picked up a commercial flight to LaGuardia.

That was the last flight of Prosperity Airways. Shortly after, they went out of business. I found out that the real reason that the primary aircraft wasn't available was that it was re-possessed by their creditors.

Marvin Bader & The Toilet

Flashback: In order to appreciate this story one must understand who and what Marvin Bader was. Marvin, a former Production Stage Manager for ABC, was rehired in 1969 as Production Manager for the 1972 Summer Olympic Games in Munich. His job was to assist in planning and to control expenses for both ABC Sports and Broadcast Engineering and Operations.

He couldn't control the above the line expenses (ABC Sports had a deep pocket in those days). However, with his penurious attitude toward living expenses of the B.O. & E. folks, he would, figuratively speaking, drive most of the BO & E personnel up a wall. Again, since the personal expenses of the Sports personnel were beyond his control, he exercised his prerogative in severely limiting any BO&E expenses that were charged to the program budget.

This he did with a vengeance. I got the impression that anything Roone Arledge or the more important sports personnel wanted, they got. Not so with BO&E. Obviously he could not limit Julie Barnathan, but everybody else was fair game. In addition, the man was insensitive to the needs of the BO&E personnel. He felt that his obligation for their personal comfort was not his obligation. This would change as time passed. I guess that he realized that there was a relationship between personal comfort and productivity.

Marvin made his first survey trip to Munich with me. We spent much time together, meals, meetings, etc. I briefed him on the progress of the project and my involvement. For the record, my assignment was the sole designer of the broadcast Center technical facilities, (See Chapter 15). Marvin's character was multi-faceted. At times he could be amusing. Our first dinner in Munich was at a fancy French restaurant. Wishing to impress me he asked the waiter to "Bring us your finest German wine". The French waiter drew himself up and replied, "There are no fine German wines!"

Our discussions covered many topics; the project, family, etc. I told him that Julie Barnathan agreed that my family could accompany me to Munich. I told him that my oldest child Ivan, who was seventeen, did not know if he wanted to accompany the family to Munich because he would "have nothing to do". Marvin said that he would hire Ivan as a daily worker, that there was a need for many "daily hires". As it turned out, at least fifty or sixty young people were hired in this fashion.

One of Marvin's first displays of insensitivity toward BO&E, particularly Joe Maltz, occurred early in the Munich Olympics project.

My family and I arrived in Munich in early July and Ivan was put to work immediately. I must say that Ivan was extremely happy with this situation. He met other young people, was doing something constructive and was earning money. As time passed, more ABC personnel arrived, some also with teenage children. Some of these youngsters were also hired to fill needed positions.

Then Jim Mckay arrived on the scene. He wanted a job for his daughter. Apparently Marvin felt that Jim's daughter would not be a "good" hire. Marvin told Jim that there were no more jobs available instead of telling the truth. I guess Jim made a fuss and Marvin went to Roone Arledge for advice. Roone said, "Simple, no relatives of ABC employees can work at the Olympics." Marvin, who to my knowledge never disagreed with Arledge, promptly fired Ivan and a few other ABC youngsters.

My son Ivan was extremely upset, as was I. In order to make it up to Ivan we arranged for him to visit a friend who had a summer job in England.

That and several other episodes soured my relationship with Marvin. However, I had a job to do. I could not let my unhappiness with Marvin affect my job performance. He could have handled this whole situation in a much different manner. After the Munich Olympics, ABC won the rights to several more Olympic games. In the back of my mind was the thought that someday, somehow, I would "Get even".

"Fast-forward" to 1980. ABC had won the rights to the 1980 Winter Olympics in Lake Placid. We were to be the Coordinating Broadcaster. Part of my duties was to design a Radio and Television Broadcast Center in conjunction with the Lake Placid Olympic Organizing Committee and the Gilbane Construction Company. This building would house all the central production and technical facilities for the Winter Games. All construction in the building would be temporary. After the games, the building would be used for a variety of Village services.

I participated in many meetings with representatives of Lake Placid and The Gilbane Building Company. Gilbane had a fine reputation having built the Smithsonian Space & Science Center in Washington, DC. The plan was to design a building to house an international broadcasting center that would be suitable for a post Olympic use.

My job was to design the ABC facilities portion of this building.

I had a pretty good idea by now of what was needed, after designing broadcast centers for three previous Olympic Games for ABC. I also knew the personal preferences of key people, i.e.: Roone Arledge, Julie Barnathan, and Marvin Bader. My task was to design a floor plan that would satisfy all.

I knew that Roone Arledge wanted to have his key people around him, be isolated from most of the other people and have rapid access to the main control room. Julie Barnathan had to have a comparable office. He wouldn't say so but as President of BO&E and an equal partner in the coverage of the games, he was entitled to the proper image. Marvin Bader had to be in the middle of the business side of the operation. He also preferred to have his back to the wall so that he could rest his head against the wall and also see who came into his office. I also had to take into account, personnel traffic flow, relationship of the studio to the videotape facilities, location of toilets, etc

Wait a minute. Location of toilets and Marvin's office. Marvin wants his desk chair against a wall. All of my grievances against Marvin suddenly surfaced. Now was the time to get even!

As the design of the facility progressed, it became apparent that the temporary men's toilet facility should be next to Marvin's office. The urinals would be on the wall behind Marvin's desk chair. Since this was to be a temporary toilet and Marvin wanted me to keep costs down, I didn't feel that it was necessary to acoustically isolate the urinals and the related water pipes.

The rest was obvious. Every time somebody flushed a urinal, Marvin would get an earful. He was furious! However, by this time, it was too late for any alterations. I had a bonus in my revenge in that the construction company, in order to save money, had cheated on the size of the drain pipes. Consequently, there were several backups of the toilet sewerage and waste water overflowed into Marvin's office.

This didn't make up for the mistreatment that I received at the hands of Marvin, but it helped. Several years later, Marvin found out about this. Boy was he furious! I remember him yelling at me, "Don't you EVER do this to me again!" Too late! I had my revenge.

Two weeks before the Winter Games were to begin, the Television Broadcast Center was a beehive of activity. Pre-Olympic interviews, film to tape transfers of material from previous Olympics and editing of assorted sequences were keeping our staff and equipment extremely busy. These processes were constantly being interrupted by momentary power failures and line voltage surges. Of course, these interruptions were wreaking havoc with our schedules and tempers were flaring. Calls to the local power company, Niagara Mohawk Power and Light, didn't help any. The power company representatives were unsympathetic.

Phil Levens and I visited the local power substation that was operated by Lake Placid to check on the ability for the town to cope with the power requirements of this major event and to maintain smooth continuity of power. We expressed our concerns. The engineer on duty sympathized with us and said that Niagara Mohawk has always treated the Lake Placid community poorly. He said that every day, when more power was required, the power company switched huge capacitors on the line. This kept the voltage from being reduced, but it caused a surge in the line voltage feeding the town and the Broadcast Center. His requests for relief from this situation to Niagara Mohawk went unanswered. The engineer told us that Niagara Mohawk had the equipment to accommodate this "surge" problem but refused to install it.

Ten days before the games were to start and before we had our emergency power in place, the power failed completely. We had no power for over 24 hours. We were told that a main transformer feeding the Village had failed and that a replacement was being shipped in by rail

Naturally, tempers were very short by then. Phil and I were being subjected to all sorts of abuse by our production people. Our ears were ringing from everybody yelling, "Do something!" We decided to find out if any progress was being made in the replacement of the defective transformer.

The town power engineer told us where the defective transformer was located and we went to check on the progress of the replacement. Sure enough, the new transformer was in place and connected into the system, but still no power. A Niagara Mohawk employee was relaxing in the sun and we asked him what the problem was. He told us that the new transformer was installed but that it was hooked up wrong. We asked him if he was taking care of the problem. "Oh no, that's somebody else's job." "Did you call that person? "No, I'm out to lunch."

On that note, we left this idiot and went back to the Broadcast Center and reported our findings to Julie Barnathan. Julie got on the telephone to call the Governor's office to see if we could get some action there. Jim Mackin, our Vice-President for Press Relations, was also in the office, and took another incoming call. He passed the telephone receiver to me and asked me to handle that call.

The caller wanted to know what the power problem was. I told him that the Niagara Mohawk people were acting like a bunch of amateurs. I described what had transpired that day. He said "thank you" and hung up. I asked Jim who it was that I was talking to. He replied that it was a reporter for some local newspaper.

Later that day, power was finally restored and we got back to the business of broadcasting. End of this problem, or so I thought.

The next morning I got a call from the reception desk. There was a delegation from the Niagara Mohawk Power Company. I figured that if I am going to meet with these people, I had better have somebody else from ABC with me. I paged Joe DeBonis, our Director of Field Operations and asked him to meet me in the Conference Room.

I ushered my visitors into our Conference Room. The delegation consisted of the Executive Vice-President, the staff Attorney and the Area General Manager. The Niagara Mohawk Vice-President proceeded to lay into me. He told me that I had slandered his company and that they were considering a defamation lawsuit against ABC. I asked him what this was all about. He replied, "Your newspaper article." I said "What article?" With this, he flung a copy of a local newspaper, the Syracuse Herald Journal, at me. I asked him if I could read this article before I respond. He agreed. I read the article, and for once, I was quoted accurately. I put the newspaper down and stated that the article was indeed accurate. I told them I said all that and was prepared to prove it.

The Niagara Mohawk Power Vice-President became flustered and his tone of voice immediately changed. I guess he realized that his company did indeed screw up and that, figuratively speaking, ABC had a louder voice than Niagara Mohawk. He apologized and stated that Niagara Mohawk had no intention of interfering with the Olympic coverage. What could his company do to assure us of getting and maintaining the proper power?

I told him, "First, get rid of those voltage correction capacitors, notify us beforehand if there are going to be any power adjustments and get some people down here that we can communicate with. He agreed to all of my requests. We had no further problems with Niagara Mohawk. In fact, they drove me nuts with all of their telephone calls to check on our well-being. The Niagara Mohawk folks didn't know who they were messing with.

Another Power Story. As in every major sporting event, as typified by the above tale, emergency power is a big MUST! The Olympic Games in Lake Placid was no exception.

The Lake Placid Olympic Organizing Committee had made arrangements with the U.S. Army to provide emergency power generators for all Olympic locations, including the Television Broadcast Center. They were state-of-the-art mobile high capacity diesel generators. My responsibility was to provide a back-up system at the Broadcast Center to utilize this emergency power when necessary.

The design was relatively simple. Niagara Mohawk power was

supplied to the Broadcast Center at a single location. It was then distributed throughout the building. We provided manual transfer switches so that if the Niagara Mohawk power failed it would be a simple matter to transfer the power source through these switches to the Army generator.

I developed a plan to coordinate the efficient transfer of power if necessary. In the event of a power failure, Technicians at key locations in the building would "power down" their locations. When I received notice from all locations that their operations were safely shut down, I would notify the electrician stationed at the Transfer Switch. He would then tell the technician stationed at the army generator to start the generator. When the generator reached full power, the technician would notify the electrician that "Power is up." The electrician would flip the power switches.

This procedure required proper communications between all concerned. The telephone company provided all the building interior hard-wired circuits. The military provided walkie-talkies" between the mobile unit and the power transfer switches location. This sounded relatively simple.

It was now time to test this "Modus Operendi". I arranged for the tests to be made one day at 6:00 AM before normal broadcast center operations would start. The test started. I established communications with all concerned. The following is the dialog that took place:

Joe Maltz to Building Electrician, "Electrician, Kill the power to the building!"

Building Electrician, "Power killed."

Joe Maltz to technicians at foreign broadcaster studios," Turn off power to all equipment!" Each studio location responds, "Equipment power turned off."

The electrician at the power transfer location would then notify the military technician, via radio to start the emergency generator.

The military technician would start the generator and then notify the electrician,

"Power coming up!" And then,

"The generator is powering down. I'll try again. "

He repeated the process

"Power coming up." Again, after a brief period,

"The generator is powering down."

He repeated this process several times. Same results. Each time the Army technician would start the power-up process, the emergency generator would fail to start.

By this time it was too late to continue the tests. There was some problem that prevented the emergency generator from completing its startup process. I did not want to interfere with the normal pre-Olympic preparations. We terminated the tests.

Later on that day, the Army technician came up with the problem and the solution. There was nothing wrong with the fuel. The problem was that the portable radio that was used for communications between our building and the emergency generator was somehow shutting down the generator. Whenever the technician "keyed" his radio, the radio would trigger the electronic circuits in the generator control mechanism. That was a generator design flaw.

The immediate problem was solved by installing a hard-wire communication circuit between the generator and the power transfer location, and discontinues the use of the walkie-talkies. The next set of tests was successful. We were now ready for any Niagara Mohawk power outages.

A few days later, when the Army technicians were testing their generator, it suddenly powered down. After some investigation it was determined that the local Olympic transportation company vehicles were communicating via radios while passing by the broadcasting center. Obviously we couldn't tolerate that. The bus company was notified and large "No Transmitting "signs were posted on the road in front of the Broadcast Center.

The importance of a properly functioning emergency power

backup was demonstrated at the recent (2013) Super Bowl game in New Orleans.

New York State Troopers to the rescue.

The 1980 Winter Olympics saw the introduction of many new production devices, including Dubner Systems graphic arts CGB-2, (Graphic Arts Generator), that produced digitized maps and bumper animations and Swiss- timing displays

Max Berry, then ABC Director of Engineering, had a special interest in making sure that this equipment was working properly. He had a longstanding relationship with Dubner Computer Systems. Keith Thompson a Dubner Systems engineer had come to Lake Placid to "fine tune" the equipment. The games started and the Dubner equipment was functioning properly so Keith decided that he could return to his home in New Jersey.

Keith left and of course soon after he left, the equipment malfunctioned.

Max asked Marvin Bader our Director of Production for help. Marvin seemed to know everyone, apparently notified the State Police, described the problem and gave them a description of Keith's vehicle who by this time was somewhere on the New York State Northway. Could they find Keith and bring him back to Lake Placid. They responded and located Keith somewhere on the highway.

Keith must have been quite surprised when he saw the State Highway patrol car roaring up behind him with flashing lights and approached Keith's VW and directed him to pull off the road. I could imagine Keith's consternation and then the ensuing conversation, "Are you Keith Thompson", "Yes sir". "You're needed back in Lake Placid". I imagine Keith was quite surprised!

Keith was escorted back to the Lake Placid Olympic Broadcast Center, where he performed his magic. End of story.

Chapter 23
Planning for 1984 Olympics

I n early 1980 I returned to New York and settled down to a relatively normal life. Then Julie called me into his office and closed the door. The ensuing conversation would have a considerable impact on my career at ABC.

Julie told me that ABC is negotiating for the U.S. television and radio rights to the 1984 Summer Olympic Games. As such we would be the Host Broadcaster. That meant that we would have to provide facilities in Los Angeles for an international broadcast center. I would have an important role to play in this endeavor.

Julie had selected the Gower Studio Complex on Sunset Boulevard as a possible location. It was a movie and television production complex located on fourteen acres in the heart of Hollywood on Sunset Boulevard. The facility had a history dating back to 1921 when it opened as The Columbia Studios under the ownership of the Cohn brothers. Julie asked me to go to L.A. and inspect the complex to determine if it was suitable for an operation of this magnitude.

With his passion for secrecy Julie told me, "Don't tell anybody about this trip". I asked, "what about Max Berry? He's my immediate boss. He has to sign my travel vouchers." Julie's response was, "Don't worry about it I'll take care of it."

Of course I told Max. Max, knowing how Julie operates, understood. No problem. He signed the travel voucher, no questions asked. Julie also instructed me, ""When in L.A. stay away from the ABC facilities, No one is to know the reason for your visit." I asked"What about Bob Trachinger, our West Coast BO &E Vice-President and General Manager?" Julie repeated, "NOBODY".

So off I went on my secret mission

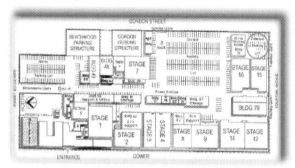

Sunset-Gower Plot Plan

As the Plot Plan indicated, The Gower Studio Complex consisted of many sound stages (studios), buildings that would support the needs of a world class Olympic operation and more than adequate parking space. After inspecting the facility I agreed that it could adequately fill the requirement of an International Broadcast Center. Of course I stayed away from the ABC Broadcast Center.

I reported back to Julie, he gave a "thumbs-up" to Roone Arledge and negotiations with the US Olympic Organizing Committee got underway.

The final negotiating sessions got under way in Los Angeles on September 10, 1980. The ABC entourage, consisting of Roone Arledge, his aides, some corporate executives and Julie Barnathan and his aides which included Joe Maltz, Manager of Central Facility Design, flew (First Class no less) to Los Angeles and were put up at the Century Plaza Hotel. The negotiating team, which certainly did not include the middle management people, entered the final round of negotiating with the US Olympic Organizing Committee, in competition with the other major TV networks.

Several middle managers were on call to crunch out budget

numbers for the various costs that go into a venture of this sort. The operation would include multiple mobile units, construction of commentator reporting facilities at many venues, television transmission networks, operating staffs at all the venues and the construction and operation of an International Broadcast Center.

That's the reason that the middle management people were there. We stayed at the Century Plaza feeding numbers to the negotiating team. The meetings started, I believe, on Wednesday September 10th and continued on Thursday and then into Friday. I was getting anxious since Saturday, September 13th was Marilyn and my 28th wedding anniversary and we had tickets for Saturday night for the "Sweeney Todd" show on Broadway. Saturday morning came and went. Finally at about 2:00 PM we got the word that ABC had secured the contract. And I was free to return home. It was too late to get home in time to make the show, but I just wanted to go home.

I told Julie and Phil that I was going to take a Red-Eye flight home that night. They both agreed that they too were ready to go home. We made first-class reservations on a TWA flight, (the airline was still flying then). Phil and I wore the usual traveling outfits, blue blazers and blue jeans. Julie wore blue jeans and a non-descript sweater. This was some dress for a vice-president of a major broadcasting company.

We arrived at the airport at about 10:00 PM, checked in and went directly to the departure gate. It was a "Zoo". Every seat was taken, travelers lying on the floor. I asked Julie if he could get us into the VIP lounge. He looked at me, nodded his head and said, "Follow me." Off we went to for the TWA VIP lounge.

There was a nice lady sitting at the desk in front of the Lounge. She greeted us and asked, May I see your VIP card?" Julie placed his ABC business card that read "Jules Barnathan, Vice-President, American Broadcasting Company", on the desk in front of her. She looked at Julie then at the card at least three times. All this time Julie was staring at her face. Finally, she said, "Welcome, go right in." Julie hiked up his trousers and said,"It works every time."

It was a nice flight home. Except I was trying to sleep and Julie kept telling me, "Eat something, we're paying for it.

Chapter 24
The move to Los Angeles

W hen ABC secured the North American rights for the 1984 Summer Olympics, it was time to put together a team. It was to be a joint venture of ABC Sports and ABC Broadcast Operations and Engineering, (BO&E).

The ABC Sports Department would be responsible for all production and programming aspects of this major endeavor.

BO&E would be responsible for all technical aspects. This included:

Neutral camera coverage of 31 Olympic events.

Commentator communication systems at each sports venue so that each participating broadcaster could provide live commentary to their home countries.

Specialized television coverage of events that the American audience was interested in.

Responsibity for the transmission of all television signals from all venues to the International Broadcasting Center.

Videotape recording and playback facilities available to all foreign broadcaster studios within the broadcast center. Assist in the design of several "Unilateral' studios where the foreign broadcasters could assemble their own programs. A central transmission facility to accommodate all of the above.

In addition we had to solve the huge logistical problem of offices, scenery shops, etc.

This was a challenge of a lifetime.

Julie asked me if I would assemble a budget for the Broadcast Center and then, when approved, supervise the design and implementation of the technical facilities.

This would require an extended on-sight presence in Los Angeles. I would receive a promotion with a commensurate salary increase. My wife and I would be relocated to L.A. And, post Olympics I would have a permanent position as a Director in the ABC West Coast Engineering Department.

In January of 1981 we sold our house in Elmont, New York and moved to Los Angeles and settled in. The plan was to remain in Los Angeles until I retired and then possibly move to the San Diego area.

The Mary Pickford Building

Previously ABC had acquired the Mary Pickford building at 1313 Vine Street to house the ever expanding staff of the West Coast operation. It was to become ABC's headquarters for the Los Angeles 1984 Olympics and would accommodate the Olympic engineering and production staff.

I was assigned a temporary office on the third floor of the building in what was the executive suite of days past, until a suite of offices were constructed on the ground floor of the building to accommodate the Olympic operation.

Why did I mention my temporary office location? Fast forward 32 years. The Academy of Motion Picture Arts and Sciences, which now owned this building, had "resurrected" the Science and Technology Council and hired Andy Maltz, my younger son as Director of the Council. His office is located on the third floor of 1313 Vine Street!

Hint of things to come

Julie chose my new job title, Director of Host Broadcasting. The Vice-President & General Manager of ABC's West Coast BO&E's Operation, Bob Trachinger objected, trying to limit my authority by specifically identifying areas where I would have authority. It took a telephone call to Julie Barnathan to settle the subject of my job title

Julie, in no uncertain terms told Trachinger that my job title is Director of Host Broadcasting.

I think that at that time a "seed" was planted in Trachinger's mind, "Get rid of Joe Maltz!"

Organization Meeting

Sometime in early 1981, the ABC 1984 Olympic Senior Staff convened in Los Angeles for the first time. We were to be introduced to corporate executives as well as to each other. Roone Arledge introduced the leaders of the ABC Sports team. In the process he announced the promotion of Marvin Bader to that of Vice-President of Olympic Production for Sports. This sort of rankled many of us who knew Marvin.

Julie Barnathan then introduced Robert (Bob) Trachinger, BO & E Vice-President & General Manager of the West Coast, who then introduced Herb Kraft as Director of Olympic Venues. Bob was extremely complementary of Herb, explaining how he, Bob, had trained Herb. Then it was time to introduce Joe Maltz.

Here were Bob's exact words, "I would like to introduce Joe Maltz, Director of Host Broadcasting. Joe, please tell us something about yourself".

Wow! What an introduction! I was somewhat embarrassed. I wasn't quite sure how to follow Bob Trachinger's laudatory introduction of Herb Kraft. I stood up, trying to figure out how to describe my background without appearing to brag. .

I got as far as, "Well, I was born at ABC" when Phil Levens interrupted me and said he will take over my introduction. He started out by saying, "With the possible exception of Roone Arledge, Joe is the most important person in this Olympic operation". He went on to present my credentials. That was some introduction! Later on I asked Phil, "Why?" He said that I deserved it. However, I knew that he also wanted to get back at Marvin Bader who wanted people to believe that he was"Mr. Olympics".

With the experience that I had gained based on four previous Olympics, in planning the technical requirements and implementing them, I forged ahead. I assembled an engineering staff and established contact with manufacturers and other providers of service for the games.

Part of my duties as Director of Host Broadcasting was to provide space and technical facilities for many foreign broadcasters. This entailed many meetings and, of course business lunches that were sponsored by ABC. Many of the broadcasters responded by hosting meals for me and my team

Chapter 25
Dining with Foreign Broadcasters

The Australian Channel 10

One of our business lunches was with the Australian Channel 10 General Manager and his staff. The General Manager, Wilf Barker, invited several members of the Host Broadcaster's staff to a lunch at a very fashionable restaurant. Everybody arrived on time at the restaurant, except for Wilf. He arrived, after a fashionable delay, in a block-long limousine. Wilf was a large man. He swept into the restaurant like a royal personage, greeting his "subjects", and took his seat at the head of the table.

He snapped his fingers requesting the wine steward and ordered, I'm sure, one of the most expensive wines available. The wine steward presented Wilf with the prerequisite sample of wine. Wilf sampled the wine, proclaimed it to be "excellent!" The wine was poured for the rest of the party. Wilf then proposed a toast, "Here's to a fine wine, good food and good friends". I couldn't resist responding with, "Well two out of three isn't bad."

Everybody had a good laugh. Except for Ed Hirst. Ed was responsible for the business affairs of the International Broadcast Center. Ed was mortified! Figuratively speaking, Ed slid under the table. One had to understand that Ed had a very limited sense of humor. What he didn't understand was that the Australians and my team enjoyed an excellent relationship. The Australians and Americans were very similar, including a terrific sense of humor. We finished the meal, which by the way, was excellent and we thoroughly enjoyed the repartee.

On the return trip to our offices, Ed berated me. "How could you do this? Insult our host when he was toasting us." I told Ed, "Please get off my back." Ed said that there was going to be a repercussion over this "insult".

About an hour after we returned to our offices, a messenger arrived with a package for me from Wilf Barker. In the package was an Australian Olympic tie with a note. "Joe, it was a delightful lunch. The only other person in town with an Australian Olympic tie is Peter Uberoth." Peter Uberoth was the head of the Los Angeles Olympic Committee. I guess Wilf enjoyed the repartee. Ed couldn't understand that good friends can tease each other.

When I made the decision to leave the Olympic team and return to New York, Wilf invited Marilyn and me to a dinner in our honor to express their thanks for the help that I had given them in their preparations for the Olympics. The dinner was attended by the entire Australian staff and included the Australian Trade Representative. The foreign broadcasters were sorry to see me leave the project.

The Japanese Television Network

I had several planning meetings with the Japanese Television Network NHK to discuss their proposed television studio. The NHK engineer, Kenkichi Tsubata spoke very little English and relied on his interpreter, a Japanese lady, Mucci Taylor. Over a period of time, the engineer, Mucci and I became friends.

Luncheon with NHK Staff

Through Mucci, Kenkichi Tsubata invited my staff and me to dinner at a Japanese restaurant. As I recall, the décor was Japanese and the waitresses were young Japanese ladies clad in typical Geisha garb. I asked Mucci to order for the group. As she gave the order in Japanese the waitress looked at her with a blank stare. She told Mucci that she didn't understand Japanese. We all had a good laugh and started a pleasant conversation. I asked Mucci about her career. She told us that she was unhappy about the role of women in Japanese society. She decided to come to America and pursue a career here. She did some modeling, (she was beautiful), and then started a business as an interpreter. Along the way she met and married an American businessman with the surname of Taylor.

When I commented that she must be a good housewife. She replied, "Oh no. I told my husband-to-be that I don't cook or do housework." Then she told us that her husband was Jewish, that she converted to Judaism and was raising their son in the Jewish faith. He was bar-mitzvah'd later that year.

At this point the fun began. I told Mucci that she was a "JAP", meaning of course that she was a Jewish American Princess. She understood and laughed but there was a look of horror on Kenkichi's face. Uh-Oh. I told Mucci that there was some explaining needed.

Mucci assured me that she will attend to this potential problem but that the explanation was an involved process. First she had to tell Kenkichi what she was going to tell him, then tell him what the expression meant and then tell him what she had said. While this was going on he had an intense look on his face. We were all wondering what was going on.

Then, suddenly he slapped his forehead and started laughing. He slapped my back. We all joined in the laughter. I had made a good friend. I guess that one can conduct business while maintaining a sense of humor.

The British Broadcasting Company

Marilyn and I were invited to dinner by many of the foreign broadcasters that I had met in the course of my involvement in many Olympics. Marilyn didn't exactly enjoy many of these dinners because the technical discussions were primarily of a technical nature which she was not familiar. In her words, "All your talk was in letters and numbers,"

However, I persuaded her to join me at these dinners because, number 1, I enjoyed her company and number 2, because she is a charming lady and my dinner companions always enjoyed her company. On this occasion, the representatives of the British Broadcasting Company (BBC) Alex Weeks invited us to dinner at Perino's, a prestigious restaurant

I explained the "letters and numbers" situation. Alex assured me that he would see to it that Marilyn would enjoy herself at the dinner. He said that Clive Potter, his lead engineer would join us at this dinner.

Marilyn and I pulled into the Perrino's parking lot in our 1977 Oldsmobile. The parking attendant parked it alongside the Rolls

Royce and Mercedes. Alex and Clive met us in the cocktail lounge and ordered drinks. Alex had a gift for Marilyn, a photo book of scenes in London and other parts of England. Included in the book was a photo of a handbag stall in Petticoat Lane, a flea market in London. Interesting coincidence; I took this photo in 1969 in Petticoat Lane of a "Shill" returning a purse tot this very same vendor.

Pettycoat Lane

In the meantime, Clive started pumping me for information about available broadcasting facilities and options for the foreign broadcasters. As I had stated before, the purpose of these dinners was to enable the foreign broadcasters and the host broadcaster to reach agreements on the facilities that we were to provide for them.

After these two independent conversations progressed for a while, I called "Time out! " Alex asked "What's wrong? " I told them, "I realize what you gentlemen are doing. You, Alex, are keeping Marilyn busy while you, Clive, are pumping me for information." Both gentlemen looked at me rather sheepishly; they were caught in the act! I proceeded to tell them, with a smile on my face, "Now that we understand each other, this is fine with me. Let's continue. Needless to say, all of us had a fine time that evening. The British and I got the needed information and Marilyn thoroughly enjoyed herself.

In 1982 Marilyn and I visited England on a business trip as guests of the BBC. Clive and his wife entertained Marilyn and me. We also were treated to the experience of attending tennis matches at the Wimbledon Stadium where we sat "Center Court".

Chapter 26
Olympic Experience Cut Short

This is a difficult chapter to write because it describes some errors in my judgment

First, some background. When I was transferred to Los Angeles, my assignment was twofold. Assemble a team to design and implement a broadcast center that was capable of supporting the 1984 Summer Olympics and to provide support for the ABC Los Angeles staff with regard as to how to host an event as important as an Olympics. I was to report to Bob Trachinger, Vice-President and General Manager of ABC's West Coast BO&E.

All went well for the first year and a half... I assembled a staff of managers and engineers and based on my past Olympic and broadcast facility experience I put together a budget for the construction of ABC's Olympic Host Broadcast Center for several million dollars. I delegated various tasks to my staff so that I could concentrate on defining the individual requirements of the foreign broadcasters.

I didn't realize that all this time, Bob Trachinger was plotting to get rid of me. I believe that his plan all along was that after the major planning was accomplished, to make my life so miserable that I would opt out of the operation. He succeeded.

In retrospect I think that he resented the fact that he was "cut out" of the initial Olympic planning and that I was involved. He wanted this to be "his" Olympics. I was in his way. Initially he had tried to limit my authority and failed.

It was then that I committed a major error in judgment. While I didn't cut my ties to Julie Barnathan, I started sending my reports to Trachinger as any good subordinate would do. During the last few months of my tenure he would complain to Julie about my job performance and that my expense vouchers were "kited". It wasn't until Julie questioned me on a particular travel voucher that I realized what Trachinger was up to. Discredit Joe Maltz!

By that time I was under intense pressure. I felt that the job wasn't worth it. One morning I confronted Trachinger. The conversation:

Joe Maltz. "I have the strong feeling that you would like to get rid of me"

Bob Trachinger. "You're correct."

Joe Maltz. "Then let's do it."

Trachinger immediately called Julie and told him that I wanted out.

Julie agreed and the die was cast. Amazingly, I felt relieved.

I spent the next few weeks preparing for my departure, completing a progress and status report that I gave to Chris Cookson, Trachinger's assistant. They both thought that Cookson would get my job and that the Olympics would be a complete West Coast operation.

That was not going to happen. I had designated, Manuel (Manolo) Romero, the Assistant Chief Engineer of The Spanish Television Network, as liaison to the participating foreign broadcasters. He was selected to replace me as Director of Host Broadcasting.

Manolo's first request was to "Get Trachinger off my back". According to Phil Levens, Trachinger was then assigned to "Checking door knobs."

I wasn't quite sure what my next job would be. Trachinger, now that his goal of getting rid of me as Director of Host Broadcast was accomplished, offered to help me get a job in ABC's local station, KABC. I was also offered a job as Chief Engineer of the Disney

Cable Channel. However, Marilyn and I thought it best to exercise my option to return to ABC New York.

My staff arranged for a farewell luncheon for Marilyn and me. They presented me with this plaque.

Joe Maltz Engineer

Later on I found out that Trachinger paid for the luncheon and even wanted to attend. My staff told him that they didn't think that was a good idea.

Chapter 27
I resume my career in New York

In January, 1983, Marilyn and I returned to New York. My job title reverted back to Manager. However since the role of Manager, Central Facilities was no longer available, my new job title was Manager, Cable Systems and Special Projects. Special Projects is sort of a catch-all phrase.

This was a period of growth for ABC. New studio facilities were opened across town. These studios had to have access to the videotape facilities in the central plant. Telco circuits were expensive. Working with manufacturers I developed a more efficient use of our broadband cable system.

However, much of that work could not be included in the category of Adventures in Broadcasting.

Director of Advanced System Planning

After some time Max Berry now Vice-President of Engineering presented me with a blank Job Description Form with the title, Director, Advanced System Planning. I was told to complete the form with a description of what I thought the responsibilities of this new position would consist of. I think that management wanted to continue using my creative talents. It turned out that this was a good decision for both the Company and me. My assignment was to assist Max Berry in his role as Vice President of Engineering and investigate new engineering innovations.

I was invited to join the Studio Standards Committee of the Society of Motion Picture and Television Engineers. As the title of the committee states, it was responsible for setting the design standards for equipment used in broadcasting. The committee consisted of engineering representatives of many broadcast equipment manufacturers, television network engineers and independent consultants. Apparently members felt that my knowledge and experience in broadcasting would be an asset to the committee. I served as Chairman of the Subcommittee on Cables and Connectors. On June 28, 1991 I was named as a Fellow of the Society and on June 8, 1992 I was honored as a Life Fellow of the Society.

The next chapter describes some of my more interesting and challenging projects in my capacity as Director of Advanced System Planning.

Chapter 28

Interesting and Challenging Projects

In 1985 NBC developed a rudimentary Affiliate Identification System, using a slide projector, which they called "Name Dropper". This system would insert, at the appropriate time, the local affiliate logo in the lower corner of the picture frame. It had many shortcomings and problems but was the only game in town.

The ABC Affiliate Relations Department asked the NBC people if ABC could use that system. The NBC response was, "No Way!" The ABC Affiliate Relations people asked our engineering department if we could develop our own system. The project was assigned to me.

After some research, I decided that we could develop a computer based electronic system that included color graphics. I won't go into any details about design, etc. Basically, this is how the system worked: The ABC Network would send out a hidden electronic signal as part of the regular network television program. At the appropriate time affiliate local stations would insert their station logo. The time and location in the picture would be determined by the network using a sophisticated computer generated process.

This was sort of a family affair. Andy, my younger son, researched and found a British Broadcasting Company (BBC) research paper that described the type of transmission protocol that would work for this system. Ivan, my older son, told me that his company, Dubner Computer Systems could design and build a system that would accomplish this. Ivan would provide the software design and Harvey Dubner's son Bob would design the hardware. The fathers, Harvey and Joe supervised their endeavors.

We had to give it a new name. The ABC Affiliate Relations Department decided to have a contest. The affiliate television station that picked the winning name received a free unit

The winning name was "Master Key". The system proved to be very successful and was installed in most of the ABC affiliate stations. Other television networks soon adopted this system.

Master Key was the basis for the affiliate identification keyed inserts in use today.

In November 1987, at the Society of Motion Picture and Television Engineers Conference, Ivan and I presented a paper on this Affiliate Identification System.

U.S Capitol Fiber Optic Installation

In early 1986 a consortium was formed by the Washington News Bureaus of the major television networks to provide a fiber optic network in the U. S. Capitol. This network would enable the networks to provide live interviews at various locations throughout the capitol building. I was assigned the job of coordinating this project.

The project was going quite well, or so I thought'

On April 23 I received a telephone call from Julie Barnathan, President of ABC Broadcast Operations & Engineering. The call went something like this:

Julie: Without any, "Hello": "I was just told that you are taking money under the table for awarding the contract for Fiber Optics cable installation in the U.S. Congress."

Joe, of course somewhat taken aback: "Julie, Do you believe this?"

Julie: "If I did, would I be making this call? You would find the lock on your office door changed when you came into work."

Joe: "I have made no special deals. Now that you believe me, can I ask you who told this to you and what did this person say?"

Julie: "Tom Murphy, the Chairman of the ABC Board of Directors. He told me that his good friend, who is a lobbyist in Congress, told him this. His son's company, an electrical contractor, bid on the job to install fiber optics cable throughout the U.S. Capitol building. His company lost the bid to another company because Joe Maltz took money "under the table.""

Joe: "Julie, you know this is not true. Would you like to hear the true story?"

Julie: "Yes. I want a full report on my desk tomorrow morning."

I'm not going to bore the reader with all the details of my five page single-spaced report. Essentially this is what transpired over a several month period:

Because of my experience with fiber optics I was asked to secure bids on a fiber cable installation to permit individual camera pick-ups throughout the capitol building and to transmit these video pictures to the networks for distribution.

After researching suitable suppliers of fiber cable, I selected four manufacturers for further consideration. They would have to supply the fiber cable and contract for its installation. I also asked the Assistant Director of Telecommunications for the Senate Sergeant-At-Arms Office if he had any contractors that he would like to recommend. (BTW, I had to buy him lunch every time that I met with him).

One of the requirements of the contract was that the manufacturers had to supply their own fiber cable. I narrowed the search to three manufacturers plus the contractor that the Sergeant-At-Arms recommended. This contractor stated that he represented a fiber cable manufacturer that he wouldn't indentify. During the period of negotiating with the prospective vendors I discovered that this contractor was asking one of the other bidders to supply him with fiber with the contractors name on it. That violated the conditions of the bid process.

After due consideration I eliminated the high bidder, (Too much profit) and the low bidder, (didn't understand the scope of the project). That left two bidders. One fiber manufacturer who had thoroughly researched the project and the contractor that the Sergeant-At-Arms had recommended

This contractor was planning on using cable supplied by the other bidder. The cable manufacturer was the low bidder. I had no problem in awarding the contract to the cable manufacturer. It was at this point that I received the telephone call from Julie Barnathan. After much discussion it was decided that I should separate myself from this project. There was too much politics involved. The ABC Director or Purchasing would take over and have the vendors resubmit their bids. The bidder that I had recommended was chosen. Of course I was absolved of any impropriety.

These fiber optic circuits from the rotunda and other locations in the U. S. capitol building are in use today. They carry the audio/video of all the interviews conducted by the news media.

It was at this time that I seriously considered retiring from ABC.

Chapter 29
ABC Retirement – New Career

In 1985 The American Broadcasting Company was purchased by Capital Cities Communications Inc., a much smaller broadcasting and publishing firm, in a deal valued at more than $3.5 billion. The new management was seeking to trim the broadcast division and was offering attractive employee buyouts. I felt that after thirty seven years with ABC, it was time to move on. Through the years, because of my experience and knowledge of the broadcast industry, many manufactures had sought my advice on new products that they might develop and market. Their representatives would take me to lunch and discuss the possibility of new products. I would gain weight and they would gain new products.

First, I needed permission from management to discuss post retirement consulting contracts with potential clients. No problem, Max Berry reported back to me that it was okay as long as I waited until the technician's union contract was approved. In the event of a strike I would be needed to operate our Master Control facilities.

I didn't want to consult full time and did some calculations. I did not want to make consulting a full time career. A "part-time" career would be fine. I would offer potential clients 20 days of consulting for a fixed fee. I would keep record of my time. So, 20 days times 4 clients would equal 80 days. I would double that for research time, total 160 days. That would leave me with 165 days of free time. Boy was I ever wrong! I would offer my consulting services to four manufactures. They all agreed to my fee and terms with handshakes, no contracts required. These contracts were honored until I actually retired.

Now I had to wait until the union contract was signed. I asked Max Berry to notify me when that happened. In August 1986, Marilyn and I were on vacation with friends in Canada when Max called and informed me of the signed contract. My first expression was, "Free at last, free at last."

I retired from ABC August 31, 1986 with a good "buyout" and a comfortable pension. It was time to look to the future.

Chapter 30
Consulting Career

I embarked on my post ABC career in September, 1986. I incorporated my consulting practice as a Subchapter S Corporation with the corporate name, Joseph Maltz Associates. Who knows, my children might join me in this endeavor.

My post-ABC would prove enriching in more ways than one. My initial four clients were:

Kings Electronics – Kings Electronics is a manufacturer of video cable connectors. My relationship with them started in 1965 during my SMAG (Chapter 12) days. At my request they developed a simple inexpensive video connector. They were happy to have my assistance in developing a series of video connection devices that would be used in the new world of high definition.

Chester Cable Company – Chester Cable is a manufacturer of specialty electronic cables. Interestingly, the company started as a manufacturer of woven rope. The same machinery was redesigned to weave wire strands for cable signal isolation. My relationship with the company dates back to my early days in the engineering department. At my request, they developed a series of multi-pair audio cables that simplified installation. They used my consulting service to help market their new products.

Catel Company - Designer and manufacturer of broadband cable products. In the late 1960.s I had helped them design equipment that was suitable for wide band television transmission. They also wanted to continue our relationship and were willing to pay for it

Dubner Computer Company – Designer and manufacturer of sophisticated broadcast graphic arts equipment. My relationship with Harvey Dubner started in 1970 when I was charged with designing a more efficient Master Control for the New York network operation. During my final days at ABC we worked together on the Affiliate Identification System. (Chapter28). Harvey wanted to continue using my knowledge of the broadcasting industry to help them develop new products.

Most of my clients displayed their products at various broadcast and cable oriented trade shows. I participated in coordinating the combined display participation of the smaller companies. Of course this required my attendance at these trade shows including the NAB (National Association of Broadcasters) each year in Las Vegas. Marilyn accompanied me to many of these events. These were indeed "Adventures".

As time permitted, I added more clients.

Electronic Design Industries (EDI) – Designer and manufacturer of sophisticated Radio Frequency receivers. In 1987 I acquired them as a Client. It was a small company owned by George Ipoli. I had met George in 1984 during my stint as Manager of Cable Systems at ABC. Under my direction George had designed an "In-House" audio monitoring system where 30 audio channels would occupy the same space as a single television channel.   We kept up our relationship after I retired. I sold two of these systems to the Radio Free Europe division of Voice of America. This involved an enjoyable trip to Munich, Germany to supervise the installation. (I never thought that I would visit Germany again.)

Missed Opportunity-Telephone Caller Diverter

Sometime in 1987 Marilyn and I were enjoying dinner, when the telephone rang. Again! Of course I answered it, thinking that it was a friend or relative. I was too curious to let it ring. The caller was another random call from a vendor or fund raiser. I thought that this is ridiculous! There must be a way to screen my incoming calls, to pass calls of those that I wish to receive and to divert unknown callers to my call answering machine.

I drew a sketch of a system whereby incoming call telephone numbers would be compared to the telephone numbers in my telephone contact list. This was in the earliest days of the telephone company "Caller ID System" whereby incoming telephone numbers could be displayed, if you rented a "Caller ID" display from the local telephone company. I would call this system Telephone Caller Diverter.

I discussed this idea with George Ipoli, the President of EDI. He said that he could design a system to accommodate this. It would require the rental of a Caller ID device from the local telephone company.

We contributed $500 each and instituted a patent search. The preliminary results came back. There were no patents or patents pending on such a device. I said, "Let's go." However George had second thoughts. He said potential users would not want to pay a monthly rental for a Caller ID service. With his refusal to design the electronics for this project, the idea died. Imagine if he had agreed to go ahead with this idea of mine.

Other Consulting Clients

Bal Electronics – An English manufacturer of sophisticated Video Monitor test equipment. The company originally started out creating the decals that you see on English Wedgewood china. In Post WWII this evolved into electronic components and then sophisticated devices. Working with BAL Electronics required several trips to England.

Allen Avionics – This Company designed and manufactured

video transmission equipment. With my assistance, they collaborated with BAL Electronics on several projects.

Reprise of my Olympic career –Almost. Canadian Television was the Host broadcaster of the 1988 Winter Olympics in Calgary, Canada. In November 1987 the Chief Engineer, Marius Morais had suddenly died. Since ABC was a participating broadcaster and had extensive experience in Olympic television coverage, Julie Barnathan President of ABC Broadcast Operations at ABC was called upon to suggest a replacement.

Apparently Julie thought that I would be a suitable replacement, because he called me at home to offer me the position of Chief Engineer of the 1988 Winter Olympics. What an honor and I could get a sizable fee for my services. That work was right up my alley. On the other hand, do I need this? Marilyn and I were preparing to drive to Florida to spend our first winter there. We would have to cancel these plans and then spend the winter in Calgary, Canada

However, I really had no desire to go back to my pre-retirement life and also, this was a way of telling Julie that he was no longer my boss. Through the years he and I had a "love-hate" relationship. He wanted his subordinates to kow-tow to him and I wouldn't. Finally, I could say "No" to him. I never regretted that decision.

The following chapters relate three of my more interesting and challenging consulting assignments.

Chapter 31
The Grass Valley Group - China Trip 1987

I n the summer of 1987, Marilyn and I were enjoying our semi-retirement in Concordia, Monroe Township, New Jersey. I was now busy with my consulting assignments. I had four clients and was quite satisfied with my workload. Then along came a once in a lifetime opportunity. An all expenses paid trip to China.

The Peoples Republic of China was named the Host for the 1990 Asian Games which would take place in Beijing. The Grass Valley Group (GVG), a manufacturer of broadcast equipment, was bidding to supply the Central China Television Network, (CCTV) with equipment for CCTV's new television broadcast center in Beijing...

GVG's competition was Toshiba and Sony. Both Japanese companies were offering "friendship", meaning free equipment. GVG couldn't hope to compete on that basis so they wanted to offer free technical expertise in the design of a world class broadcast center. They felt that I could supply that technical expertise. So did I.

I supplied GVG with a resume of my broadcast credentials which they transmitted to the authorities in Beijing via the GVG's agent in Hong Kong. CCTV was sufficiently impressed with my background to invite GVG representatives and me to Beijing, to make a presentation.

I prepared a one hundred page document, which was in essence, a

"How to Design and Build a World Class Broadcast Center" manual, complete with time frame schedules. I bound this material in a plain black binder. GVG changed the binder to one of their distinctive binders and the Hong Kong agents, Advanced Communication Equipment Ltd (ACE) promptly rebound the manual in a binder with their company Logo.

In November of that year I accompanied Pete Montana and Dan Wright, the GVG President, to Beijing to make a presentation to the Chinese authorities. We met the President of the Hong Kong agency in Beijing and then presented my document to the Chinese.

An interesting note; Chinese Nationals were not permitted in the hotel that we stayed at. Guards were stationed in front to assure this.

The meeting with the Chinese broadcasters was most interesting. It was held in a large room that was furnished with comfortable armchairs around the perimeter of the room. Between each armchair was a small side table. The room and the setting reminded me of the pictures that I had seen of Chinese heads of state greeting American dignitaries.

After we had been seated, little Chinese ladies, dressed in traditional oriental garb, paddled in and served tea. The meeting started. Since we spoke no Chinese and the Chinese wouldn't acknowledge if they spoke English, the translations of the introductions were long and drawn out. Mr. Pang, our Hong Kong representative, introduced Dan Wright who gave a broad overview of our proposal. This was followed by Pete Montana who made a very laudatory introduction of me. As I had stated, all of our statements had to be translated.

Finally, it was my turn. I had to give a dissertation on what it takes to plan a world class international broadcast center. We had prepared several copies of my manual. I had to go through it page by page, making short statements so that the translations could take place.

The Chinese seemed very interested. Of course they were

noncommittal. Details were discussed as to how this plan could be affected. But somehow I knew that we were being milked for information. We left the manuals with the Chinese. I'm certain that they would translate my manual, use it as a guideline and then go for the manufacturer that would offer the most "friendship".

After the meetings were concluded and a formal banquet we were able to tour the city visiting the usual tourist sites, including Tiananmen Square.

Remember, this was in 1987 Beijing was typical of a closed society. It reminded me of Moscow in 1961. The only hint of Western culture was a Kentucky Fried Chicken restaurant. Most of the people were dressed in traditional Chinese garb.

After a few days of sightseeing we flew to Quangzhou in Southern China. What a difference between two cities. The following descriptions are not meant to be judgmental.

Informal dinner in Quangzhou

There were obvious differences in personal freedom between

Quangzhou and Beijing. Quangzhou was a whole other story. It was bustling with activity. There was modern construction going on all over the city. The people were dressed in bright colors, a pleasant mix of eastern and western cultures.

In Quongchong, we met with officials and engineers from the Southern Television Network to carry on our discussions in English and tried to help us with the Chinese translations. Their engineers' main concern was with intraplant communications. I did my best to acquaint them with some of our western technology. They seemed very appreciative and invited our team to a cocktail party and banquet that evening.

There were many toasts

Dan Wright and I were treated as guests of honor. Dan is a rather quiet, almost boring individual. I can be quite a party person. The Photo attests to the good time had by all. I distributed cigars to all. It was a most enjoyable evening. Missions' accomplished. We prepared to return home.

We drove across the river to Hong Kong for the trip home.

Mr. Pang, the president of ACE, our Hong Kong distributor, requested that I spend some time at his Hong Kong office to brief his engineers on our meetings with the Chinese. This meant that I would have to reschedule my return flight to New York. The only seats available were in first class. Dan said "go for it".

One of the ACE representatives and I left the group at the Hong Kong airport and drove into the City. It was time for lunch and he asked me what I would like to eat. After all the Chinese delicacies, I wanted some western food. We went into a local hotel and I had a corned beef sandwich on rye. Delicious. Interesting tidbit. The restaurant menu stated that kosher meals were available.

After lunch, I met with the engineers from the ACW Group and gave them a resume of my presentation.

That chore taken care of, Michael Pang, ACE's president asked me if I would like to do some shopping, since Hong Kong was famed for its bargains. I wanted to buy something for Marilyn, but what? Michael suggested a silk blouse. Terrific, but where? Perhaps one of the fancy tourist shops. Nope. Michael said, "Let's go to a department store." Fine. He took me to one of the local stores where only Chinese is spoken. I picked out, with Michael's linguistic help, a beautiful silk blouse that Marilyn still wears. I'm sure that if I bought it at a tourist shop I would have paid much more for it.

Our next stop on our shopping tour was to shop for imitation Rolex watches. I followed Michael through a pushcart market that was reminiscent of old time Belmont Avenue in Brownsville, Brooklyn. I put my wallet in my front pocket for obvious reasons.

Finally, we ended up in front of a men's clothing stall. A young Chinese man had an open folding stack table in front of him. On the table were photos of what appeared to be Rolex watches. I asked Michael, "Why photos?" Michael replied that it is against the law to sell the rip-offs of designer watches in Hong Kong. OK. So I picked out one ladies watch and one men's watch from the photos. The salesman turned around and started rummaging through the pockets of the men's suits hanging behind him. Some clothing store! He picked out some watches and Michael carefully examined each one. He rejected several for various reasons, bent hands and other flaws. He told me, "Don't take any "gold" watches, the gold flashing wears off too quickly." He finally "accepted" three watches. He picked well. Many years later, the watches are still working. He also told me that it's against the law to export these watches from Hong Kong. I had to hide them in my luggage. So much for my shopping. I promised Marilyn that I owe her a shopping expedition in Hong Kong. Some day.

It was time for dinner. I told Michael that I would like to eat in a restaurant that served local not "tourist" food. I wanted to be the only westerner in the room. I also asked him to order for me. Why travel six thousand miles and eat food that I can get in a local American "Chinatown" restaurant.

Michael did indeed take me into a local neighborhood restaurant. I was the only westerner in the room. He ordered a variety of foods; the main course was some variety of fowl. The waiter put down knives and forks. I told Michael that this wasn't necessary. I would use what the locals use. He said this is what the locals use. He said that they are not stupid. They knew a good thing when they see it.

Michael dropped me off at my hotel and said that he would pick me up in the morning for the trip to the airport. One comment about the hotel; the bagels and lox for breakfast were great.

My flight home in First Class was fantastic. Six thousand miles and many hours of being pampered were not too difficult to take. I made one adjustment. I set my watch to Eastern Standard Time and tried to set my sleep hours to my home time. It worked pretty well.

Epilogue. Grass Valley did not get the contract. Toshiba did. But I had a fantastic experience.

Chapter 32
Expert Witness

ABC used many new States-Of-The- Art electronic devices during the 1980 Winter Olympics. One of these innovations permitted five separate videos to be displayed on one screen. This new device was manufactured by a company called Qantel (no u after q). ABC used this piece of equipment to great advantage in displaying multiple television images.

Subsequently, the Ampex Corporation, a major broadcast equipment manufacturer sued Qantel for patent infringement. Ampex alleged that the Qantel company, a subsidiary of Abacus, Ltd., was using the Qantel 5000 Plus multi-image display device that Ampex had developed. There would be no case If Qantel could prove that the device was used at the 1980 Winter Olympics which was prior to Ampex filing for the patent,

Years later, early in 1989, Philip Bennett, an executive of the Qantel Company called Max Berry, my former boss at ABC and asked him for assistance in proving that ABC used this device at in 1980. Max recommended that he call me.

In August of that year Karl Limbach, a Patent Attorney, contacted me and asked if I could provide consulting assistance in this lawsuit. They wanted me to provide research and evidence to prove that this device was indeed used at the 1980 Winter Olympics long before Ampex filed a patent. I was told that hundreds of millions of dollars were involved. I agreed to provide this service after some negotiating over my consulting fee.

Several weeks later, I was contacted by William Gilbrath, an attorney from the New York law firm of Fish and Neave, who were representing Ampex in this lawsuit. He asked if I would provide the same services for them. I replied that I was already hired by the law firm representing Qantel. He said that that's okay; I could work for both firms. I disagreed and refused their offer.

I spent several months researching and obtaining documents and drawings that would prove Qantel's case. My many years at ABC were paying off. The folks in the ABC Engineering Library were very cooperative in providing original drawings.

Early in October, I received another telephone call from William Gilbrath. He told me that they wanted me to give a deposition regarding my work on this case. I said fine and asked if they could take the deposition in a hotel in Cranbury, near my home. He agreed.

So much for their agreement to have an amiable deposition. I was served with a subpoena to appear at a deposition hearing on Friday, October 27th, 1989 in Manhattan and to bring all pertinent documents.

I called Karl Limbach and informed him of the subpoena. He responded that he and an attorney from the litigation firm would attend the deposition hearing and that they would like to meet with me on the evening before.

After discussing the situation with Marilyn, I called Karl Limbach and told him that I would like them to put me up at their hotel so that I would not have to make two trips to Manhattan from my home in central New Jersey.

Karl agreed and asked me to make a dinner reservation for three at a restaurant in Manhattan. I asked, "What price range?" He replied "The best and most expensive restaurant in town." I did some research and selected the second most expensive restaurant in town. I have since forgotten the name.

I assembled a thick folder of documents and drawings that my research had uncovered and brought them with me to New York.

I met Karl and Kurt Taylor, the attorney from the litigation firm of Hopkins and Taylor. Over dinner we reviewed what my responses to the Ampex attorneys' questions. The "gist" of it. Before answering any question, get my attorneys approval to answer. Keep the answers short. Don't volunteer any additional information. I thought that this would be quite interesting.

I don't remember anything about the hotel other that it was expensive, $300.00 for the night in 1989.

At 10 AM the next morning we were ushered into Hopkins and Taylor's conference room on the 40th floor of the building housing their offices. It reminded me of a scene from L.A. Law (which was popular at the time.) There was an array of the plaintiff's attorneys accompanied by a stenographer on one side of the table. (Remember, there were hundreds of millions of dollars at stake). On the opposite side of the table was Karl Limbach the Patent Attorney, Joe Maltz, and Kurt Taylor the Litigation attorney.

The attorneys were all properly dressed, shirt and tie, business suits. I had decided to show that I was not "awed" by all this, so I wore casual sport clothing, no tie.

The questioning started. I identified my background and credentials. After each question by one of the plaintiff's attorneys I would turn to each of the defense attorneys and asked for their permission to respond. I responded as briefly as possible.

I was asked to turn over copies of all of my research. I think that this is called disclosure. I looked at my "advisors", they nodded yes. I said that it would take some time to copy all the documents and drawings and that I would expect to be reimbursed for the expense incurred. Of course they agreed.

Later that year I was told that Ampex lost the case.

Chapter 33
Videoplex

B y 1988 my list of consulting clients had been reduced to EDI and Videoplex. Videoplex was owned by an entrepreneur, Marty Horak. Marty's sole product was a device that combined up to 16 live images into one video signal that could be displayed on a monitor

One unique use of this device that unfortunately didn't "sell' was to use a four picture version for use by Opticians. The idea was for the customer to select several pairs of eyeglass frames while wearing their old eyeglass's and then record four separate images while wearing each eyeglass frame. The customer would then put on their original eyeglasses and then make a selection by viewing the video display of the customer wearing each of the four frames. We installed a prototype of this device in a Lenscrafter Opticians store. It didn't sell. We had much more success selling 16-image devices to several television networks.

Videoplex was my last consulting client. This relationship continued until 1996 when we moved to our retirement home in Florida.

Chapter 34
Retirement - REALLY

By the middle of 1991, I had shed all of my clients with the exception of Videoplex and even that was "spotty". I realized that I was really enjoying my retirement and didn't have time for the consulting business.

My broadcast career at ABC lasted thirty seven years; add to that another five years of consulting for the industry, for a total of forty two years. It was time to segue to a new career, that of retirement.

Looking back, it was really quite an adventure in broadcasting for this kid from Brooklyn. As part of my job I covered a sporting event in Moscow, Russia, a manned space flight, four political conventions, four plus Olympics as well as many other unique experiences.

During this period in my life, I was involved in many new broadcast innovations, experienced overseas travel and met many interesting people both here and abroad. And as a bonus, my adventures in my consulting career were quite different from those during my ABC years. I had expected to just advise manufacturers on new broadcast products. Little did I know that I would be involved in a much broader range of activities.

Postscript

In the summer of 2003 Marilyn and I visited our son Ivan and his wife Elyse in Pleasanton, California. Ivan was employed by Pinnacle Systems as a software engineer. He invited me to visit and tour

Pinnacle's facility in Mountain View, CA. I met Mark Sanders, the president of the company, who I had done business with when he worked for the AMPEX Company.

When I described my involvement with my community computer club, he asked if I would give some presentations on behalf of Pinnacle Systems and describe their video editing systems. I agreed. He asked me what my consulting fee was. I told him that a gift of a laptop computer would be fine.

Back home in Florida I introduced the Pinnacle Video Editing System to the residents of Palm Isles and Palm Isles West. As a result of this association with Pinnacle Systems I created a Media Transfer Center in the community clubhouse. I instruct residents how to transfer 8mm film and videotape to DVD's, as well as 35mm slides to CD's. I also belong to the Science & Technology Club

I keep in touch, vicariously, with the communications world through my children.

Ivan is a software engineer with Google, working in the YouTube division in Mountain View California.

Cindy Maltz Glenn is the Technology Chairman in her school in San Antonio, Texas.

Andy is the Director of the Science & Technology Council of the Academy of Motion Picture of Arts & Science in Los Angeles.

I hope that you enjoyed sharing My Adventures in Broadcasting.